SAN DIEGO

MADE EASY

Europe Made Easy
Travel Guides

Andy Herbach
Karl Raaum

Europe Made Easy
Travel Guides

www.eatndrink.com

SAN DIEGO MADE EASY
Andy Herbach and Karl Raaum
First edition 2021
ISBN: 9798564008044

Acknowledgments
Maps from www.eatndrink.com
Thanks to our editors Trish Medalen
and Brenda McCormack
All photos from Karl Raaum, Shutterstock,
Wikimedia Images and Pixabay

ABOUT THE AUTHORS
Andy Herbach is the author of the *Eating & Drinking* series
of menu translators and restaurant guides, including *Eating
& Drinking in Paris, Eating & Drinking in Italy, Eating &
Drinking in Spain and Portugal*, and *Eating & Drinking in
Latin America*. He is also the author of several travel guides,
including *Palm Springs Made Easy, Paris Walks, Europe Made
Easy, Paris Made Easy, Amsterdam Made Easy, Berlin Made Easy,
Barcelona Made Easy, Oslo Made Easy, French Riviera Made Easy*,
and *Provence Made Easy*.

Karl Raaum has contributed to all of the *Europe Made Easy*
travel guides and is the co-author of *Palm Springs Made Easy*.

The authors reside in Southern California.

You can e-mail corrections, additions, and comments to
eatndrink@aol.com or through
www.eatndrink.com.

TABLE OF CONTENTS

MAPS

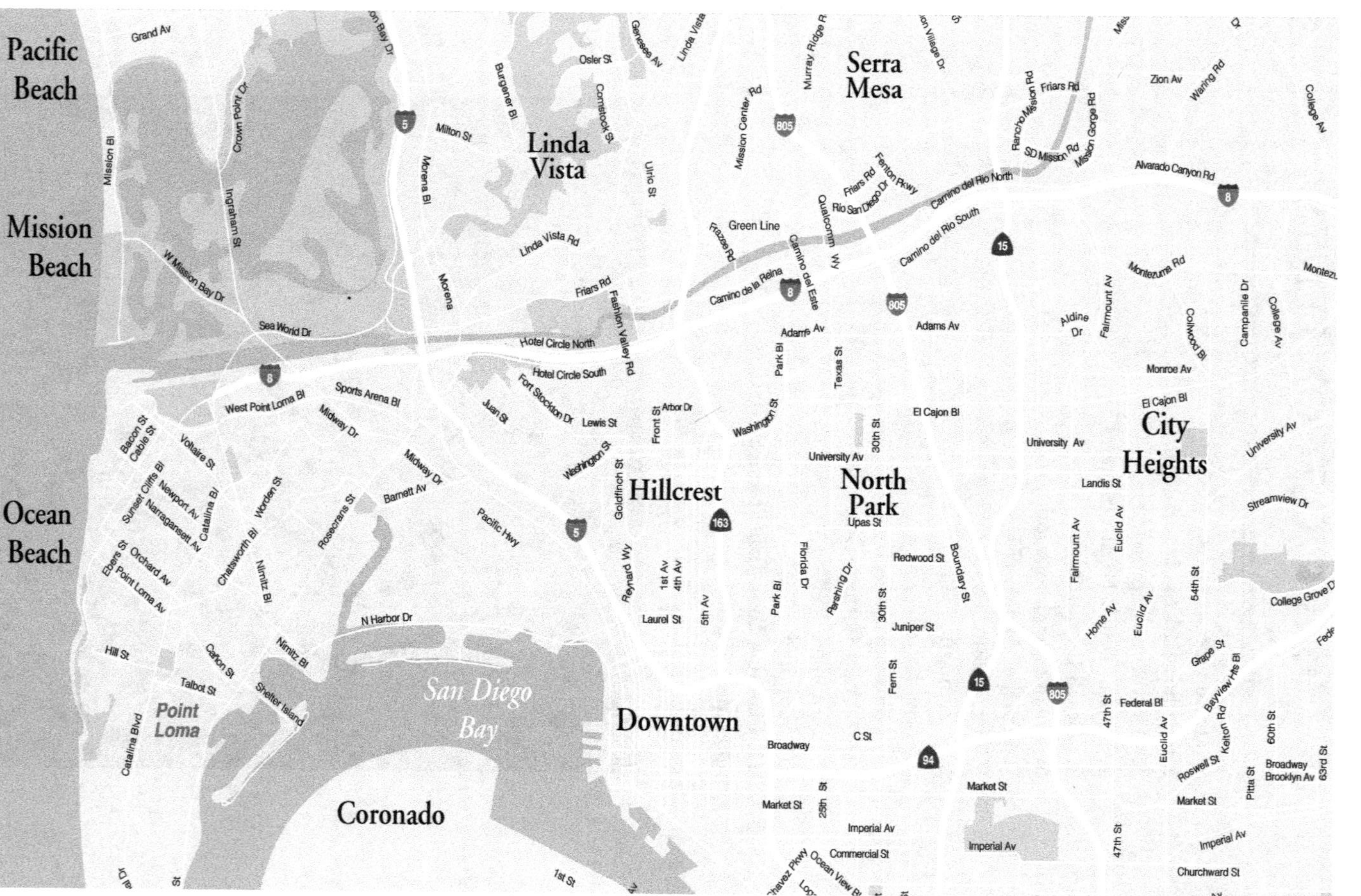

Pacific Beach
Mission Beach
Ocean Beach
Point Loma
Coronado
San Diego Bay
Downtown
Hillcrest
North Park
City Heights
Serra Mesa
Linda Vista
Grand Av
Crown Point Dr
Ingraham St
Mission Bl
W Mission Bay Dr
Sea World Dr
Burgener Bl
Osler St
Comstock St
Milton St
Morena Bl
Morena
Genesee Av
Linda Vista
Ulric St
Linda Vista Rd
Mission Center Rd
Murray Ridge Rd
Serra Mesa
Rancho Mission Rd
Friars Rd
SD Mission Rd
Mission Gorge Rd
Zion Av
Waring Rd
College Av
Alvarado Canyon Rd
Friars Rd
Fenton Pkwy
Rio San Diego Dr
Camino del Rio North
Camino del Rio South
Green Line
Frazee Rd
Qualcomm Wy
Camino de la Reina
Camino del Este
Montezuma Rd
Campanile Dr
College Av
Aldine Dr
Fairmount Av
Colwood Bl
Friars Rd
Fashion Valley Rd
Hotel Circle North
Hotel Circle South
Adams Av
Adams Av
Park Bl
Texas St
Monroe Av
El Cajon Bl
El Cajon Bl
Fort Stockton Dr
Lewis St
Juan St
Arbor Dr
Front St
Washington St
30th St
University Av
University Av
University Av
Landis St
Streamview Dr
West Point Loma Bl
Sports Arena Bl
Midway Dr
Midway Dr
Barnett Av
Rosecrans St
Washington St
Goldfinch St
Upas St
Florida Dr
Pershing Dr
Redwood St
Boundary St
Fairmount Av
Euclid Av
54th St
College Grove Dr
Bacon St
Cable St
Voltaire St
Sunset Cliffs Bl
Newport Av
Narragansett Av
Catalina Bl
Chatsworth Bl
Worden St
Nimitz Bl
Pacific Hwy
Reynard Wy
1st Av
4th Av
5th Av
Laurel St
Park Bl
30th St
Juniper St
Fern St
Home Av
Euclid Av
Grape St
47th St
Federal Bl
Ebers St
Orchard Av
Point Loma Av
Hill St
Carlon St
Talbot St
Nimitz Bl
Shelter Island
N Harbor Dr
Catalina Blvd
Broadway
C St
Market St
25th St
Market St
Imperial Av
Commercial St
Ocean View Bl
1st St
Euclid Av
Bayview Hts Bl
Kelton Rd
Roswell St
Federal Bl
Market St
47th St
Imperial Av
Imperial Av
Pitta St
60th St
Broadway
Brooklyn Av
63rd St
Churchward St
8
5
805
15
163
94

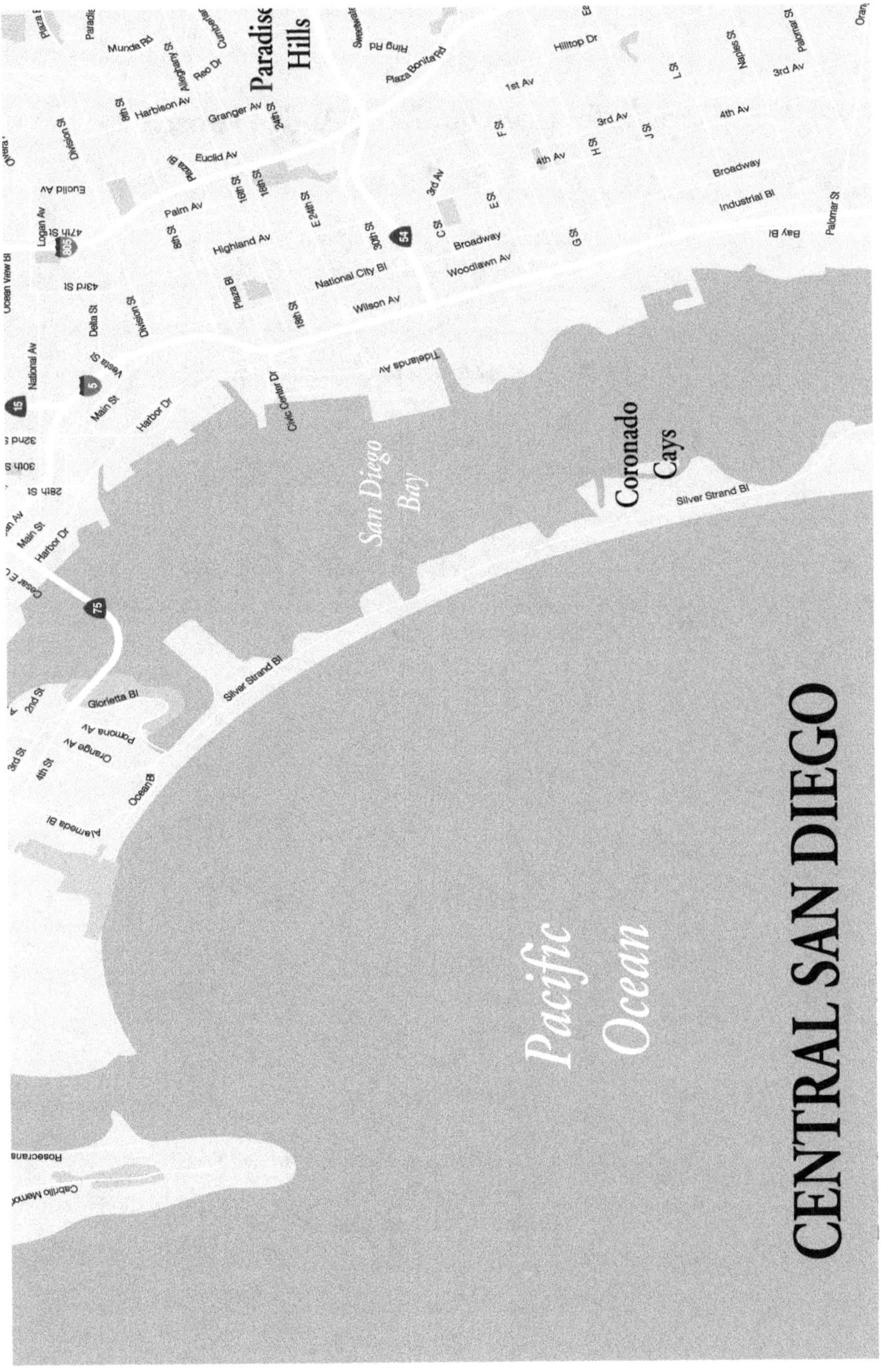
CENTRAL SAN DIEGO
Pacific
Ocean
San Diego
Bay
Coronado
Cays
Silver Strand Bl
Ocean Bl
Alameda Bl
Orange Av
Pomona Av
Glorietta Bl
Harbor Dr
Main St
Civic Center Dr
Tidelands Av
National Av
Wilson Av
National City Bl
Woodlawn Av
Highland Av
Palm Av
Euclid Av
Broadway
Industrial Bl
Bay Bl
Palomar St
Hilltop Dr
Plaza Bonita Rd
Division St
Harbison Av
Granger Av
Rosecrans
Cabrillo Memor

Reviews for travel guides by Andy Herbach

•

"...an opinionated little compendium."
Eating & Drinking in Paris
~ New York Times

"Everything you need to devour Paris on the quick."
Best of Paris
~ Chicago Tribune

"an elegant, small guide..."
Eating & Drinking in Italy
~ Minneapolis Star Tribune

"Makes dining easy and enjoyable."
Eating & Drinking in Spain
~ Toronto Sun

"Guide illuminates the City of Light."
Wining & Dining in Paris
~ Newsday

"This handy pocket guide is all you need..."
Paris Made Easy
~ France Magazine

"Small enough for discreet use..."
Eating & Drinking in Paris
~ USA Today

"It's written as if a friend were talking to you."
Eating & Drinking in Italy
~ Celebrity Chef Tyler Florence

1. Introduction

We couldn't think of one good reason to visit laid-back **San Diego**. Or just one, at least. For instance:

The weather is practically perfect. Then you have beautiful Balboa Park, with its many museums, gardens, art galleries, performance spaces—and the world-famous, spectacular San Diego Zoo—to consider. There's snorkeling in La Jolla Cove, and hiking far above the breathtaking coastline. Feel like feeding the dolphins at SeaWorld? Or how about a lazy day at the beach, followed by a night on the town?

So that's the dilemma: There are so many things to see and do in San Diego that it might seem overwhelming. But this concise little pocket guide—including insider tips on restaurants, cafes, and shops—will help you plan your trip with confidence. However short your stay, it's all you'll need to make your visit enjoyable, memorable… and easy!

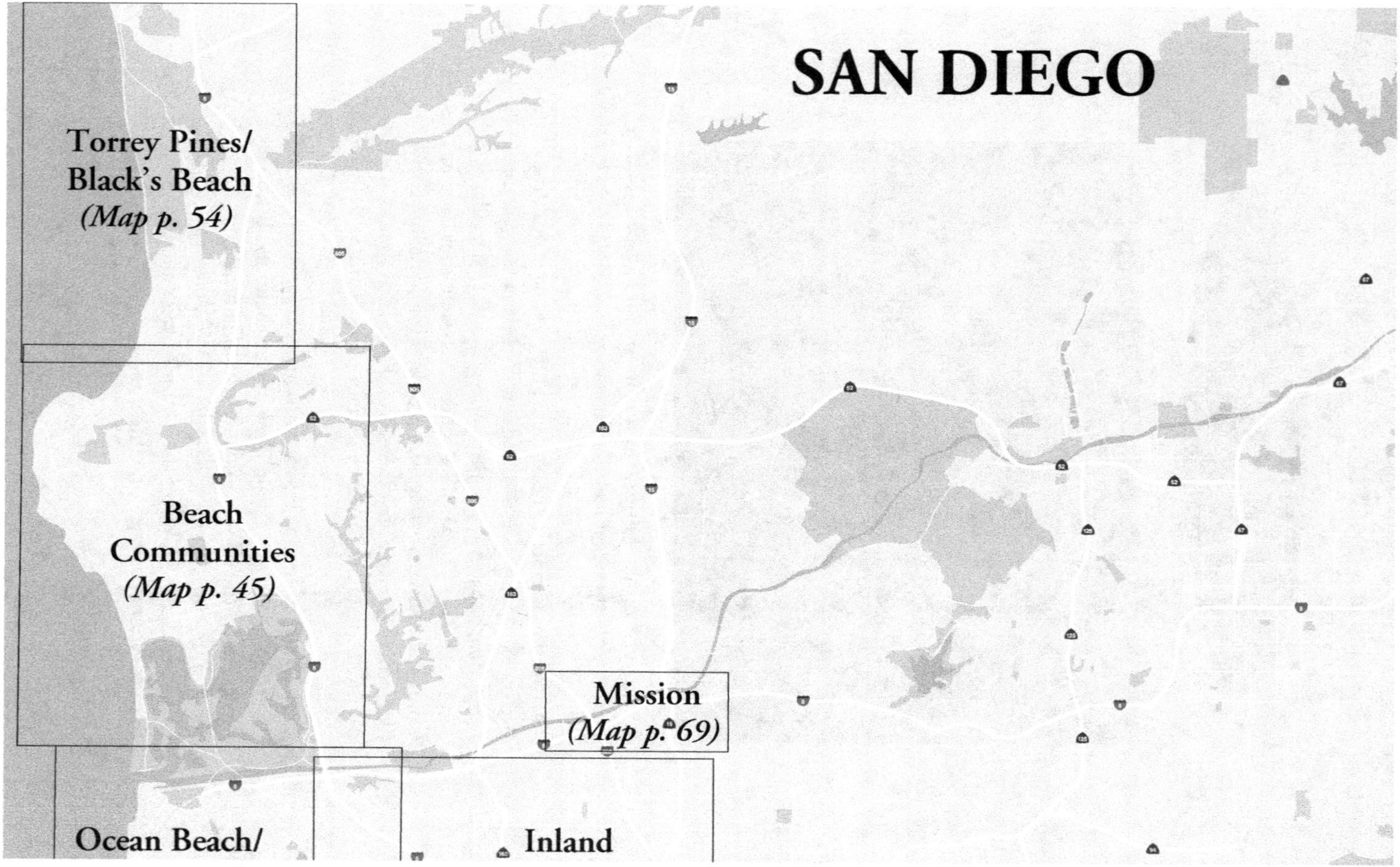

SAN DIEGO

Torrey Pines/
Black's Beach
(Map p. 54)
Beach
Communities
(Map p. 45)
Mission
(Map p. 69)
Ocean Beach/
Inland

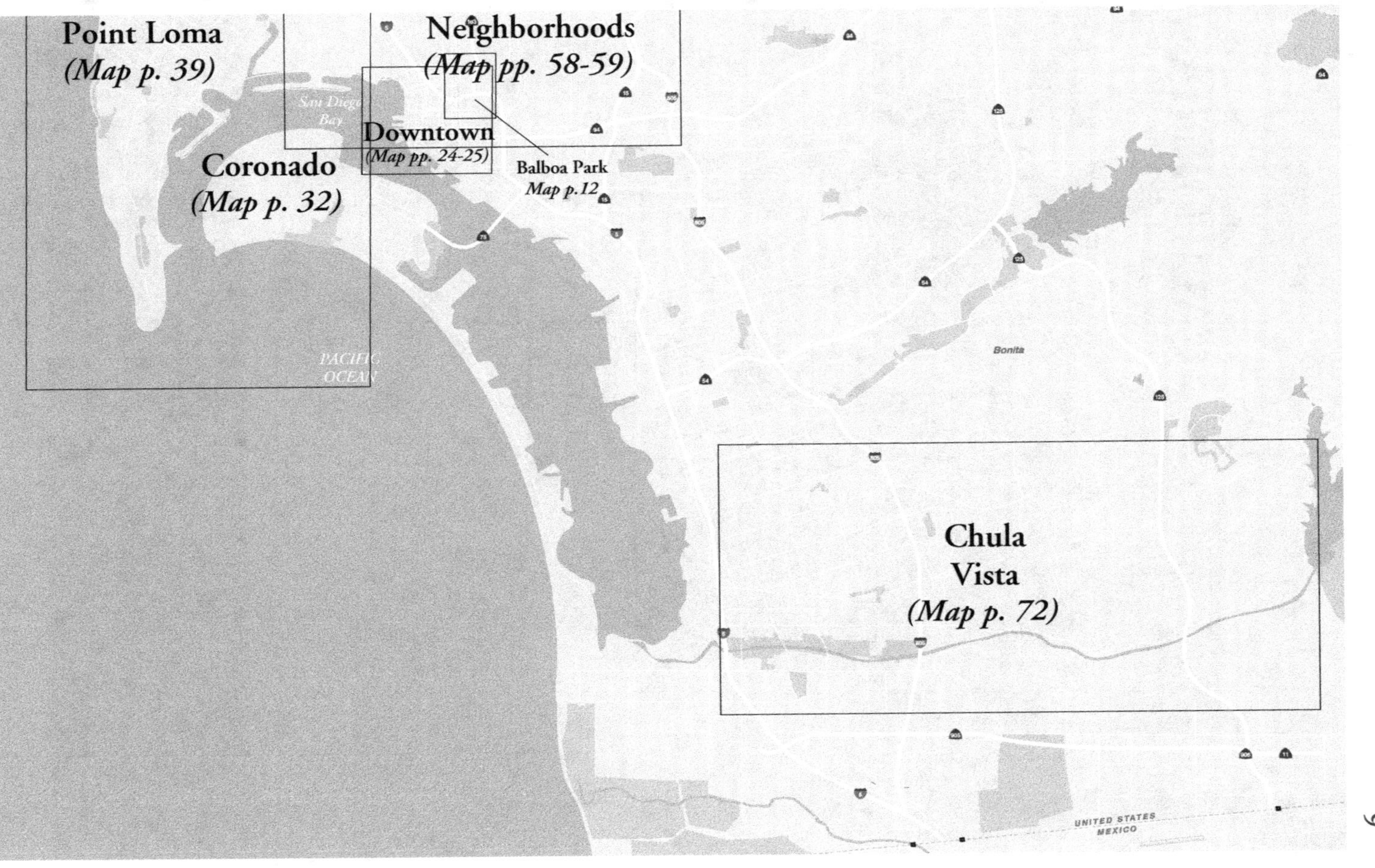

Point Loma
(Map p. 39)
Neighborhoods
(Map pp. 58-59)
Coronado
(Map p. 32)
Downtown
(Map pp. 24-25)
Balboa Park
Map p.12
Chula
Vista
(Map p. 72)
San Diego Bay
PACIFIC OCEAN
Bonita
UNITED STATES
MEXICO

COVID-19

At the time of the publication of this book, there was a national health emergency. Many of the sights and establishments were temporarily closed or operating under reduced hours. It would be wise to check the websites of the sights and establishments for updated information before your visit.

2. Balboa Park

- Museum of Us
- Museum of Photographic Arts
- San Diego Museum of Art
- San Diego Air & Space Museum
- Mingei International Museum
- Timken Museum of Art
- San Diego Model Railroad Museum
- San Diego Natural History Museum (The Nat)
- San Diego Zoo
- Botanical Building
- San Diego Art Institute
- San Diego Automotive Museum
- The Gardens of Balboa Park
- Fleet Science Center
- Japanese Friendship Garden
- Centro Cultural de la Raza
- Other Attractions in Balboa Park
- Veterans Museum and Memorial Center
- Comic-Con Museum

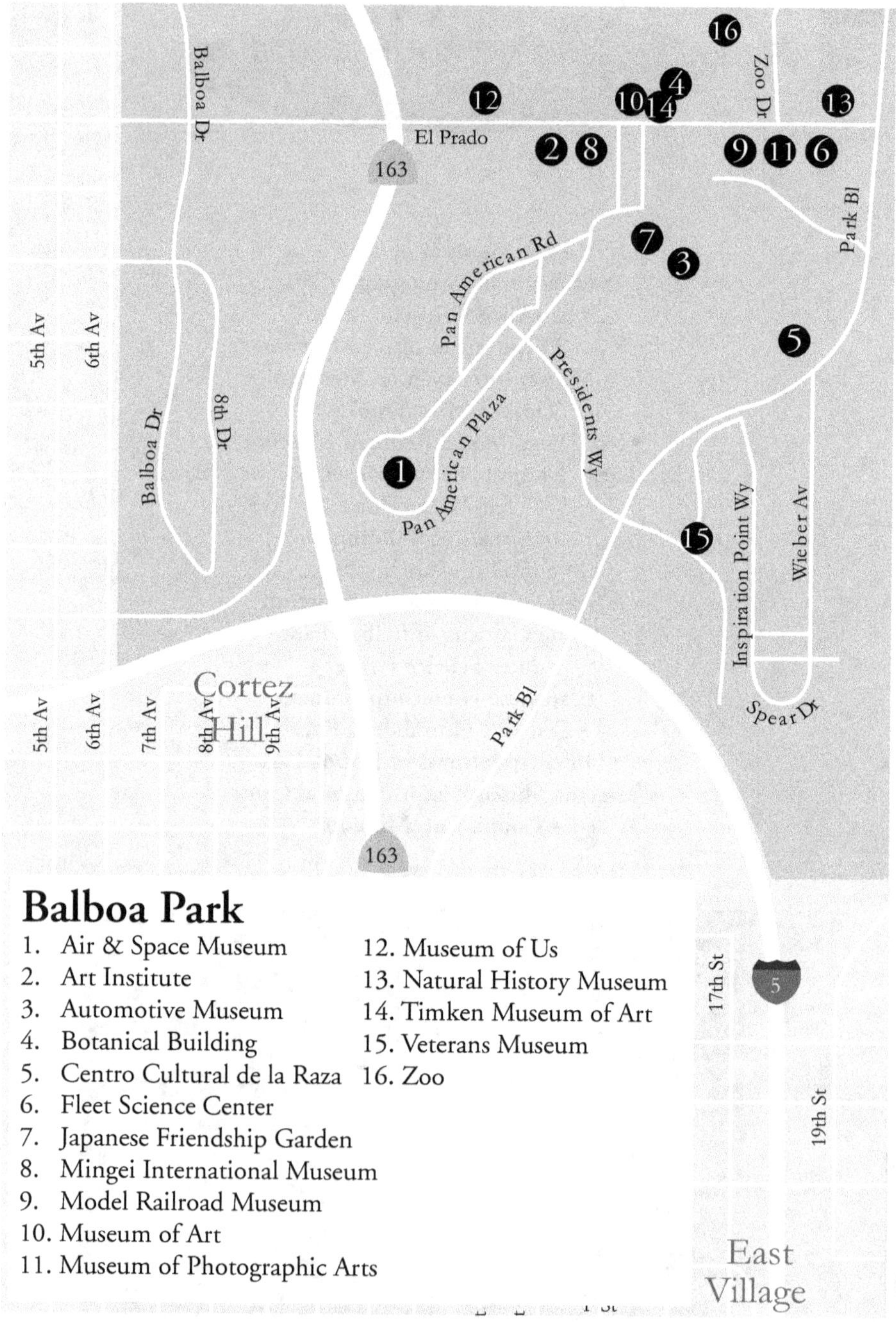

Balboa Park

1. Air & Space Museum
2. Art Institute
3. Automotive Museum
4. Botanical Building
5. Centro Cultural de la Raza
6. Fleet Science Center
7. Japanese Friendship Garden
8. Mingei International Museum
9. Model Railroad Museum
10. Museum of Art
11. Museum of Photographic Arts
12. Museum of Us
13. Natural History Museum
14. Timken Museum of Art
15. Veterans Museum
16. Zoo

BALBOA PARK
The fantastic Balboa Park is 1,200 acres filled with gardens, paths, important museums, and architectural landmarks. This is the cultural center of the city. The park was the site of the Panama-California Exposition in 1915 and the 1935 California Pacific International Exposition. The main entrance to the park is Cabrillo Bridge, which dates back to the 1915 exposition. A wide promenade runs through the park and is lined with buildings in the richly ornamental Spanish Colonial Revival style. The world-famous San Diego Zoo is here along with 17 museums and cultural organizations. www.balboapark.org.

Museum of Us
The former Museum of Man is now the Museum of Us. The museum complex is located in four buildings built for the 1915 exposition (the historic buildings of the California Quadrangle). The museum itself is located in the ornate California Building with its landmark tower. This anthropology museum displays exhibits featuring Native American culture of the region, significant Mayan artifacts, and the largest collection of Egyptian antiquities in the USA. One of the museum's prize possessions is an ancient Egyptian child's coffin. Interactive exhibits seek to get the visitor to understand the science, history, and experience of race in the country. An interesting museum in a lovely setting. *Info*: 1350 El Prado. Tel. 619/239-2001. Open daily 10am-5pm. Admission: $13, ages 6-17 $10, under 6 free, over 62 and students with identification $10. museumofus.org.

Museum of Photographic Arts
Now that so many of us have smartphones, we can take a picture whenever we want, and photography has become an important part of our daily lives. This museum, with descriptions in both English and Spanish, has a permanent collection of over 9,000 images and videos. An impressive museum of lens-based art. *Info*: 1649 El Prado. Tel. 619/238-7559. Open Tue-Sun 10am-5pm. Open until 8pm on Fri from Memorial Day to Labor Day. Admission: Donation. www.mopa.org.

San Diego Museum of Art
The building that houses this museum is a work of art itself. It's designed in the plateresque style with a heavily ornamented door. The museum has a large collection of Spanish art, including works by El Greco, Goya, Murillo, Ribera, Velázquez, and Zurbarán. The museum's collection of Italian masters includes Canaletto, Pittoni, Giotto, and Veronese. Also represented here are works from the Northern European School, including paintings by van Dyck, Rubens, and Hals.

One collection includes 48 German Expressionist paintings and drawings, including pieces by Klimt, Dix, and Münter. Overall highlights include:

- *Woman Combing Her Hair* by Renoir
- *Fleurs (Bouguet)* by Matisse
- *El Marques de Sofraga* by Goya
- *Infanta Margarita Teresa in a Blue Dress* by Velázquez
- *The Vision of Saint Anthony of Padua* by Pittoni

Info: 1450 El Prado. Tel. 619/232-7931. Open Mon, Tue, Thu, Fri, and Sat 10am-5pm, Sun noon-5pm. Closed Wed. Admission: $15, $10 ages 65 plus and military, $8 college students, under 17 free. www.sdmart.org.

San Diego Air & Space Museum
California's air and space museum is an affiliate of the Smithsonian Institution. The Apollo 9 Command Module from 1969 is here, along with historic aircraft and a GPS satellite. On display are artifacts from aviation and space pioneers like the Wright Brothers, Amelia Earhart, Charles Lindbergh (including a replica of his "Spirit of St. Louis"), Buzz Aldrin, and Neil Armstrong. The museum is big on interactive exhibits aimed at children, such as flight simulators and a 3D movie theater. *Info*: 2001 Pan American Plaza. Tel. 619/234-8291. Open daily 10am-4:30pm. Admission: $19.95, ages 3-11 $10.95, 2 and under and active military free. Reduced admission $16.95 for seniors, veterans, and students. sandiegoairandspace.org.

Mingei International Museum

Contemporary folk art and crafts are showcased at this museum dedicated to the art of the people (mingei) from throughout the world. No old-world masters here, but interesting examples of contemporary artists with no formal training. The museum believes that everyday items and materials can be objects of great interest and beauty. Not your ordinary art museum. *Info*: 1439 El Prado. Tel. 619/239-0003. At the time of publication this museum was closed for renovations. www.mingei.org.

Timken Museum of Art

California museums tend to have a focus on contemporary art, but this interesting museum has an incredible collection of old master paintings, sculpture, and tapestries. There are over 60 major works featured here. You'll find art by Rembrandt, van Dyck, Murillo, and Rubens. Zubarán's *St. Francis in Meditation* is worth the visit alone. A collection you would expect in a major European city. An added bonus is the wonderful collection of U.S. art like the work of John Singleton Copley. *Info*: 1500 El Prado. Tel. 619/239-5548. Open Tue-Sat 10am-4:40pm, Sun noon-4:40pm. Closed Mon. Admission: Free. Timkenmuseum.org.

Model Railroad Museum

The world's largest model railroad museum has miniature replicas of the California railway system. This 28,000-square-foot museum is a collector's dream. Among the exhibits here are four huge layouts of railways of the Southwest. There's a gallery of toy trains and a Lionel display. A must for model railroad lovers (and there are a lot of them!). *Info*: 1649 El Prado. Tel. 619/696-0199. Open Tue-Fri 10am-4pm, Sat and Sun 11am-5pm. Closed Mon. Admission: $12.50, ages 4-11 $6, seniors 65 plus $9. sdmrm.org.

San Diego Natural History Museum (The Nat)

Travel from the time of dinosaurs to present day at this interactive museum. There are five floors of exhibits and a giant-screen 3D theater. The permanent exhibits include:
• *Skulls*: Featuring 200 fascinating animal skulls.

- *Fossil Mysteries*: A journey through Southern California's prehistoric past.
- *Coast to Cactus*: Highlighting the region's biodiversity.
- *Extraordinary Ideas from Ordinary People: A History of Citizen Science:* Explores the work of naturalists with the theme that you do not need to be a scientist to participate in science.

Info: 1788 El Prado. Tel. 877/946-7797. Open: Tue-Sun 10am-4pm. Closed Mon. Admission: $19.95, age 62 plus/military/students $16.95, ages 3-17 $11.95, 2 and under free. sdnhm.org

San Diego Zoo

There are some fabulous museums and sights in Balboa Park, but the highlight and most famous is this zoo. Home to more than 3,500 animals, the zoo is known for its cageless and open-air habitats. It's huge and extremely popular with over four million visitors each year. Oh, and there are those pandas, too. It's one of the few zoos in the world to have bred giant pandas. The incredible Australian Outback exhibit lets you feel like you're down under experiencing all the interesting animals there (including those adorable koalas). The Africa Rocks exhibit lets you get up close to baboons and penguins. This museum does a great job of letting you experience nature in a fun and interactive way. *Info*: 2920 Zoo Drive. Tel. 619/231-1515. Open daily 9am-6pm. Admission: $60, ages 3-11 $50, under 3 free. sandiegozoo.org.

Botanical Building

Built for the 1915 exposition, the Botanical Building is perhaps the most interesting and lovely sight in the park. Facing the building is a lily pond and lagoon. One of the largest lath structures in the world, the Botanical Building has more than 2,100 plants with a collection of orchids, ferns, palms, and tropical plants. Don't miss a stroll through this extraordinary structure. *Info*: El Prado (adjacent to the Timken Museum of Art). Open Fri-Wed 10am-4pm. Closed Thu. Admission: Free.

San Diego Art Institute

This art institute exhibits contemporary art from local artists. It's located in the "House of Charm" (built for the 1915 exhibition), which has 8,000 square feet of display space. *Info*: 439 El Prado. Tel. 619/236-0011. Open Tue-Sun noon-5pm. Closed Mon. Admission: Donation. www.sandiego-art.org.

San Diego Automotive Museum

Love cars? Started by a group of car collectors is the 1980s, this museum has exhibits that feature vehicles from throughout the world. There's also a large motorcycle exhibit (heavy on Harley-Davidson products). An interesting exploration of the history of vehicles. *Info*: 2080 Pan American Plaza. Tel. 619/231-2886. Open daily 10am-5pm. Admission: $12. Age 64 plus, military, and students $8, ages 6-15 $6. Under 6 free. sdautomuseum.org.

THE GARDENS OF BALBOA PARK

Balboa Park is home to some fantastic gardens. Each has its own theme and character. All are free and open daily.
Here are some of them:

1935 Cactus Garden

Cacti and succulents. Behind the Balboa Park Club, 2144 Pan American Road W.

Alcazar Garden

Modeled after the gardens of Alcazar Castle in Seville, Spain and planted with 7,000 annuals. Just west of the Mingei International Museum.

Australian Garden

Native plants from and which were donated by Australia. End of the Gold Gulch Trail.

California Native Plant Garden

36 drought-tolerant California native plants. West end of the tennis courts at 2201 Morely Field Dr.

Casa del Rey Moro Garden

Designed for the 1935 California Pacific International Exposition and influenced by the Moorish gardens of Ronda, Spain. Adjacent to the House of Hospitality.

EthnoBotany Children's Garden

Organic herb, fruit, and vegetable garden. 2100 Park Blvd.

Inez Grant Parker Memorial Rose Garden

1,600 roses of more than 130 varieties on three acres. East side of Park Blvd. across the pedestrian bridge adjacent to the San Diego Natural History Museum.

Palm Canyon

450 palms (58 species) of palm trees. Pan American Plaza across from Spreckels Organ Pavilion.

Trees for Health Garden

An educational garden promoting the value and uses of medicinal plants. On the corner of Balboa Dr. and Quince St.

Zoro Garden

A butterfly garden containing plants needed for the complete life cycle of butterflies. Between the Fleet Science Center and the San Diego History Center.

Fleet Science Center

The Fleet is home to the world's first IMAX Dome Theater. Science, from outer space to inside the human body, is explored through more than 100 interactive exhibits. Great destination for kids. Among the highlights is *The Young Explorer*, featuring stations with age-appropriate computer games that teach math, science, and reading skills. *Info*: 1875 El Prado. Tel. 619/238-1233. Open Mon-Thu 10am-5pm, Fri 10am-8pm, Sat and Sun 10am-6pm. Admission: $20, ages 3-12 $17. www.fleetscience.org.

Japanese Friendship Garden

This garden sits on 12 acres in the heart of Balboa Park. It features a bonsai exhibit, koi ponds, azaleas, ornamental plants, black pines, and a moon-viewing deck. The friendship garden connects San Diego and its Japanese sister city Yokohama. The design is based on Japanese landscape techniques adapted for the Southern California climate. This tranquil space is a lovely destination. *Info*: 2215 Pan American Rd. Tel. 619/232-2721. Open daily 10am-6pm. Admission: $12, 65 plus/students/military $10, under 6 free. niwa.org.

Centro Cultural de la Raza

Located in a former water tower painted with colorful murals, this cultural center showcases Latino, Chicano, Mexican, and Indigenous art. Rotating exhibits feature theater, dance, music, film, and video performances. *Info*: 2004 Park Blvd. Tel. 619/363-1372. Open Tue-Thu noon-4pm. Admission: Suggested donation $5. centrodelaraza.com.

OTHER ATTRACTIONS IN BALBOA PARK

Balboa Park Carousel

This 1910 carousel features hand-carved animals. Adjacent to the San Diego Zoo. Tel. 619/232-2282. Open Sat, Sun, and school holidays 11am-5:30pm (daily in the summer). Admission: $3. www.balboaparkcarousel.org.

Balboa Park Miniature Train

Operated by the zoo, this train takes you on a short ride through parts of the park. The train station is located outside the zoo's exit. Mid-June to Labor Day daily 11am-6:30pm. The rest of the year Sat and Sun 11am-4:30pm. Admission: $3. www.sandiegozoo.org.

Cabrillo Bridge

A beautiful way to enter the park. Built for the 1915 exhibition, it was the first cantilevered, multiple-arched bridge to be built in Southern California.

El Cid Statue

The Statue of El Cid, erected in 1930, honors a Spanish knight and warlord in medieval Spain. Located at the entrance to the Plaza de Panama.

House of Pacific Relations International Cottages

These cute cottages were built for the 1935 exposition and showcase national traditions of many countries. Open Sat and Sun noon-5pm. To the west of Spreckels Organ Pavilion. www.sdhpr.org.

Marie Hitchcock Puppet Theatre

This is the longest continuously running puppet theater in the U.S. 2130 Pan American Plaza. Memorial Day to Labor Day showtimes Wed-Sun 11am, 1pm and 2:30pm. Winter showtimes: Wed-Fri 10am and 11:30am, Sat and Sun 11am, 1pm, and 2:30pm. Admission $5, $4 seniors and military, under 2 free. balboaparkpuppets.com

Marston House

One of California's finest examples of the Arts and Crafts movement, the Marston House was constructed in 1905. It's known for its lovely garden and its walking tours of San Diego's neighborhoods. 3525 7th Avenue. Tel. 619/297-9327. Admission for walking tours begins at $15. www.sohosandiego.org.

San Diego History Center

Established in 1928, the oldest historical organization on the West Coast highlights the history of San Diego. It's known for its interesting fine arts collection. 1649 El Prado. Open daily 10am-5pm. Admission: Free. www.sandiegohistory.org.

San Diego Mineral and Gem Society

Mineral, gem, and fossil specimens from around the world. 1770 Village Place. Open daily 11am-4pm. Admission: Free. www.sdmg.org.

Sefton Plaza

This lovely plaza features several bronze statues including that of horticulturist Kate Sessions, often called the "Mother of Balboa Park." She is credited with bringing many of the plants in the surroundings to the park. Located near the park's west entrance on Laurel Avenue.

Spanish Village Art Center

200 local artists have set up shops in a replica of a Spanish village that was built in 1935. Located between the zoo and The Nat. Open daily 11am-4pm. www.spanishvillageartcenter.com.

Spreckels Organ Pavilion

The star of this pavilion is the Spreckels Organ given to the city in 1914 for the Panama-California Exposition. It's the largest outdoor pipe organ in the world and has more than 5,000 pipes ranging in length from 32 feet to inches. Pan American Place. Sunday concerts at 2pm. Mid-Jun-Aug concerts on Mon at 7:30pm. Admission: Free. www.spreckelsorgan.org.

The Old Globe

Built in 1935, this performing arts venue is modeled after Shakespeare's Old Globe in London. It continues to host performances. 1363 Old Globe Way (across from the Museum of Us). Admission varies by performance. www.theoldglobe.org.

WorldBeat Center

This center promotes and preserves African, African-American, and other Indigenous cultures of the world through dance, music, art, and technology. Housed in one of the colorfully painted former water towers. 2100 Park Blvd. Hours and admission depend on the exhibit. www.worldbeatcenter.org.

Veterans Museum and Memorial Center
Located in the former chapel of the Naval Hospital, this museum is dedicated to honoring veterans. Exhibits feature World War I, World War II, Pearl Harbor, the Korean War, Vietnam, Desert Storm, and Women in the Military. The collection includes memorabilia, artifacts, artwork, and uniforms. San Diego has a rich military history and it's celebrated here. *Info*: Chapel Rd. Tel. 619/239-2300. Open Wed-Sun 10am-4pm. Closed Mon and Tue. Admission: $5, $4 veterans and seniors, $2 students, under 12 and active military free. www.veteranmuseum.org.

Comic-Con Museum
For 50 years, San Diego has hosted one of the biggest, most popular comic and popular art conventions in the world. The 1935 Federal Building has been converted into the Comic-Con Museum. Comics and popular arts are featured through events, exhibits, and programs. Not just about comics, the museum will also explore video games, tabletop games, animation, and film and television. *Info: Coming in 2021.*

Eating and Drinking in Balboa Park
There are several options for dining and refreshments in the park. Here are a few recommendations:
Alaska Airlines Flight Path Grill $-$$
If you're visiting the Air & Space Museum, this outdoor restaurant serves hamburgers, hot dogs, pizza, salads, wraps, and sandwiches. Watch the airplanes on the flight path to and from San Diego's airport. *Info*: 2001 Pan American Plaza. Tel. 619/234-8291 x124. www.sandiegoairandspace.org.

Panama 66 at the San Diego Museum of Art $$
Located in the Museum of Art's sculpture garden, this gastropub serves farm-to-table fare. Try the *charcuterie* plate. Known for its selection of beer from the city's craft breweries. *Info*: 1450 El Prado. Tel. 619/696-1966. Open Sun-Thu 11am-3pm, Fri and Sat 11am-7pm. www.panama66.com.

The Prado at Balboa Park $$-$$$
Indoor (whimsical decor) and outdoor (large patio) dining at this restaurant located in the House of Hospitality. California cuisine, like green pea and asparagus risotto, is served at the restaurant or you can opt to eat and drink at the bar, which has a lighter menu of sandwiches, salads, and tacos. *Info*: 1549 El Prado. Tel. 619/557-9441. Open Mon and Tue noon-3pm, Wed, Thu, and Sun 11:30am-5pm, Fri and Sat 11:30am-4pm. Reservations required for dinner. www.cohnrestaurants.com/theprado.

3. Downtown/ Coronado

- USS Midway Museum
- Maritime Museum
- New Children's Museum
- San Diego Central Library
- Firehouse Museum
- Petco Park
- Museum of Contemporary Art San Diego (MCASD)
- Eating & Drinking Downtown
- Coronado Bridge
- Hotel del Coronado
- Coronado Museum of History and Art
- Eating & Drinking in Coronado
- Barrio Logan
- Old Town

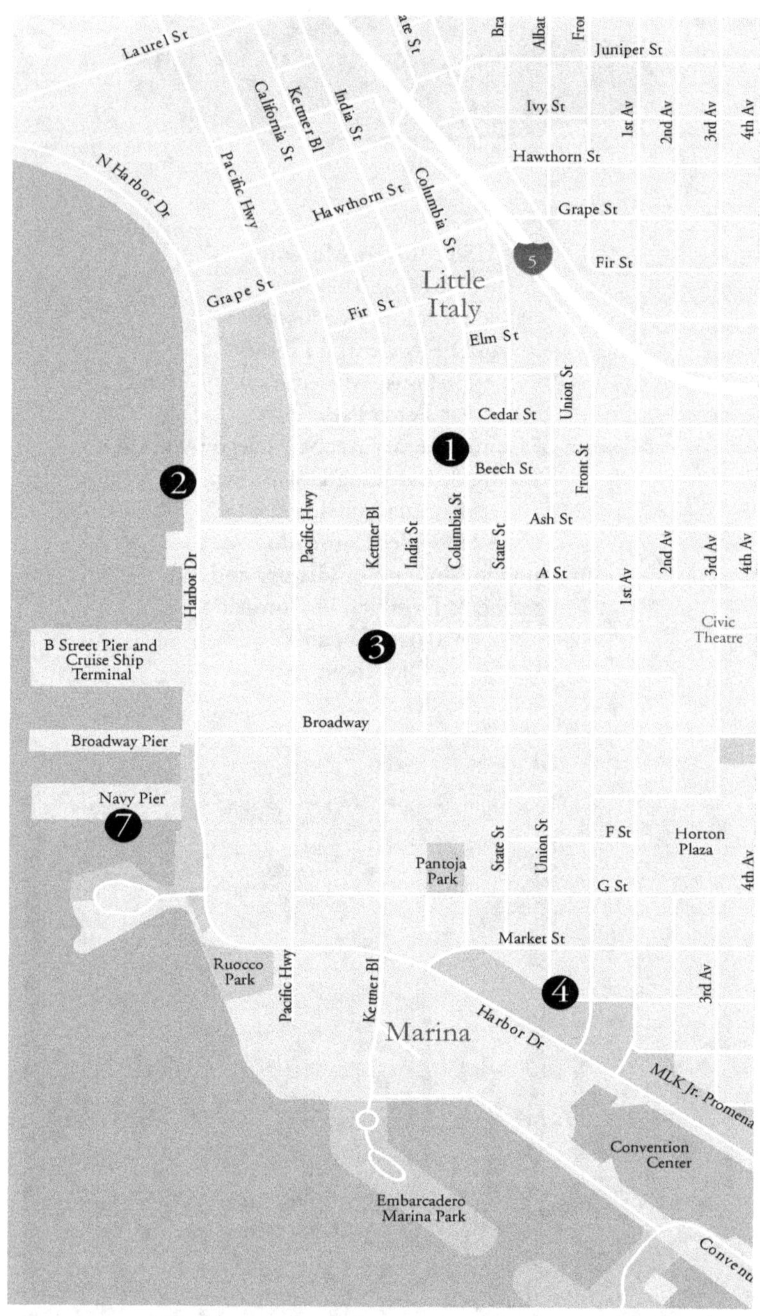

Laurel St
California St
Ketmer Bl
India St
Columbia St
Pacific Hwy
N Harbor Dr
Hawthorn St
Grape St
Fir St
Little Italy
Elm St
Union St
Juniper St
Ivy St
Hawthorn St
Grape St
Fir St
1st Av
2nd Av
3rd Av
4th Av
5
Cedar St
Beech St
Front St
Pacific Hwy
Harbor Dr
Kettner Bl
India St
Columbia St
State St
Ash St
A St
1st Av
2nd Av
3rd Av
4th Av
Civic Theatre
B Street Pier and Cruise Ship Terminal
Broadway
Broadway Pier
Navy Pier
7
State St
Union St
F St
G St
Horton Plaza
4th Av
Pantoja Park
Market St
Ruocco Park
Pacific Hwy
Kettner Bl
Marina
Harbor Dr
4
3rd Av
MLK Jr. Promena
Convention Center
Embarcadero Marina Park
Conventi
1
2
3

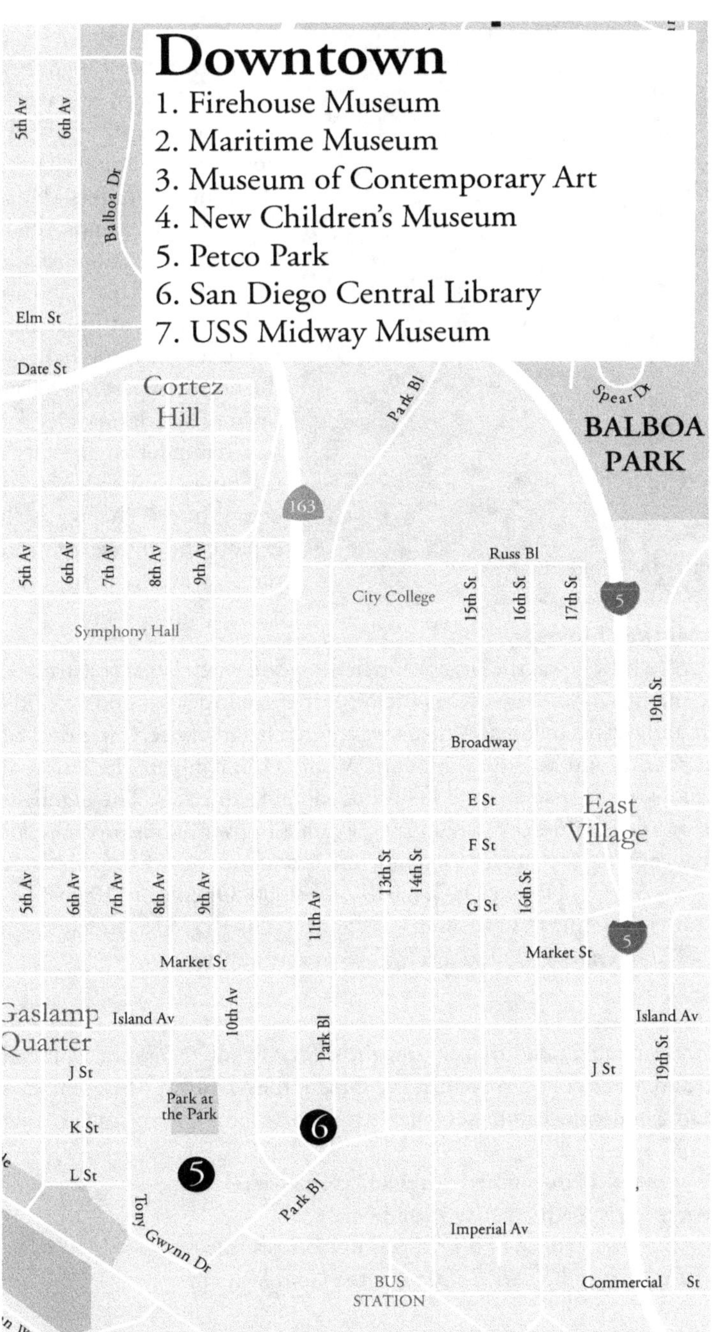
Downtown
1. Firehouse Museum
2. Maritime Museum
3. Museum of Contemporary Art
4. New Children's Museum
5. Petco Park
6. San Diego Central Library
7. USS Midway Museum
5th Av
6th Av
Balboa Dr
Elm St
Date St
Cortez Hill
Park Bl
Spear Dr
BALBOA PARK
163
Russ Bl
City College
15th St
16th St
17th St
5th Av
6th Av
7th Av
8th Av
9th Av
Symphony Hall
19th St
Broadway
E St
East Village
F St
13th St
14th St
16th St
5th Av
6th Av
7th Av
8th Av
9th Av
11th Av
G St
Market St
10th Av
Market St
5
Gaslamp Quarter
Island Av
Park Bl
Island Av
19th St
J St
J St
Park at the Park
K St
6
5
L St
Tony Gwynn Dr
Park Bl
Imperial Av
BUS STATION
Commercial St

DOWNTOWN

Downtown San Diego isn't just skyscrapers, it's a collection of unique neighborhoods. Gaslamp Quarter is home to hotels, bars, restaurants, and clubs. You'll find Petco Park, home of the Padres baseball team, in East Village. Dine at an Italian restaurant in Little Italy on the northern part of Downtown. The Marina District is a reminder of the city's important connection to the ocean. In this chapter, we'll explore the diverse sights of the Downtown area.

USS Midway Museum

The USS Midway was the largest ship in the world when it was constructed at the end of World War II. This aircraft carrier could accommodate 4,500 sailors and weighs 64 tons. When it was retired from service, it was docked in the marina and became a museum. Visitors can compare the bunks of the sailors to the spacious and luxurious captain's quarters. The highlight is the massive flight deck, which is now home to over 30 restored aircraft and helicopters. You might also enjoy the experience of a flight simulator ($8). *Info*: 910 N. Harbor Dr. Tel. 619/544-9600. Open daily 10am-5pm (last admission 4pm). Admission: $26, age 62 plus $22, $18 students, age 6-12 $12, veterans $10, under 6 free. www.midway.org.

Maritime Museum

Like the aircraft carrier that houses the USS Midway Museum, you can board and tour a collection of historic ships at the Maritime Museum. This interesting museum features several boats. Here are some that you can explore:

- *Star of India*, 19th-century merchant sailing vessel
- *Berkeley*, early 20th-century steamboat
- *HMS Surprise*, replica of a 17th-century British frigate
- *USS Dolphin* and *Soviet B-39*, from the Cold War era

When touring these ships and submarines, you realize how the quarters are extremely confined and claustrophobic. Another museum that brings to mind the importance of the military to the history of the city. *Info*: 1492 Harbor Dr. Tel 619/234-9153. Open daily 9am-5pm (until 6pm on Sat and Sun). Admission: $20, $15 ages 62 plus and 13-17, $10 ages 12 and under. www.sdmaritime.org.

New Children's Museum

Learning in a fun way! This hands-on museum let kids think, create, and play with displays that teach them about art and the world around them. The Clay Studio and the Paint Studio lets them experience art with their own hands. An example of the interactive exhibits here is the Mattress Room that allows kids to jump on more than 40 mattresses and 160 pillows that look like vehicle tires. Fun for children of all ages. *Info*: 200 W. Island Ave. Tel. 619/233-8792. Closed Tue. Admission: $15.50, $10 ages 65 plus and military. www.thinkplaycreate.org.

San Diego Central Library

You wouldn't think that this would be worthy of an entry in a travel guide for tourists, but this public library is not like other libraries in the U.S. Opened in 2013, this innovative space has 500,000 square feet over nine stories and holds more than one million books. There's a special section for kids and the 3-D printing lab is just one of the interesting exhibits here. The view from the rooftop deck alone is worth a visit. *Info*: 330 Park Blvd. Tel. 619/236-5800. Open daily 9:30am-5:30pm. Closed some Sundays. Admission: Free. www.sandiego.gov/public-library.

Firehouse Museum

You can explore the history of firefighters at this special-interest museum located in a former fire station in Little Italy. Vintage fire trucks, horse carts, and firefighting equipment are featured here, and you can view the sleeping quarters of the firefighters. There's a special exhibit on firefighters who joined the 9/11 effort, including a piece of the World Trade Center from New York. *Info*: 1572 Columbia St. Tel. 619/232-3473. Open Thu-Sun 10am-4pm. Admission: $4. www.sandiegofirehousemuseum.com.

Petco Park

Built in 2004, this stadium is home to the San Diego Padres of Major League Baseball. It's in the heart of Downtown where the Gaslamp District and East Village converge. It's also near the Convention Center. The park was built around the brick Western Metal Supply Company building, a historic landmark. The stadium also hosts concerts and soccer events. There are great views of San Diego Bay and the city's skyline. If you climb to the upper deck, you'll have a stunning view of the Coronado Bridge. The area around the park has turned into a destination for dining and bar hopping even when there is not an event. *Info*: petcoparkevents.com and mlb.com/padres.

Museum of Contemporary Art San Diego (MCASD)

The main branch of this museum is located in La Jolla. The La Jolla location is currently closed for renovation and expansion. There are nearly 5,000 pieces of post-World War II art in the museum's collection. Some of the collection and exhibits are shown at the Jacobs and Copley Buildings located Downtown. Among the art are works by Christo (*Wrapped Package*), Ellsworth Kelly (*Red, Blue, Green*), and Franz Kline (*Untitled, 1953, black and white gouache on paper*). *Info*: 1100 Kettner Blvd. Tel. 858/454-3541. Hours vary so check the website. Admission: $10, seniors and students $5, ages 25 and under and military free. www.mcasd.org.

Eating & Drinking Downtown

Ballast Point Brewing $$

This tasting room and restaurant is in the heart of Little Italy. There are over 50 beers on tap (try the Sculpin IPA) and dining both inside and outside on the large patio. San Diego is known for its craft breweries and this is a great introduction. Eclectic menu features blue cheese duck nachos, vegan burger, and grilled fish sandwich. *Info*: 2215 India St. Tel. 619/255-7213. Open daily 11am-10pm. ballastpoint.com.

Donut Bar $

Forget everything that you thought you knew about donuts. This breakfast joint in the Gaslamp Quarter is very popular. You'll love their selections, from the Red Velvet Cake Donut to the Triple Chocolate Threat Cake Donut. Down it with house-made strawberry milk. *Info*: 631 B Street. Tel. 619/255-6360. Open Mon-Thu 10am-3pm, Fri 7am-3pm and 5pm-10:30pm, Sat 8am-3pm and 5pm-10:30pm, Sun 8am-3pm. www.donutbar.com.

The Mission $$

Mexican and American cuisine at this East Village spot. Interesting choices for breakfast like Desayuno Burrito (tortilla filled with potatoes, eggs, cheese, beans, and chipotle cream) and the Zen Breakfast (scrambled egg whites, brown rice, and braised tofu). Great coffee and bread baked on the premises. *Info*: 1250 J St. Tel. 619/232-7662. Open daily 7am-3pm. www.themission.com.

Herb & Wood $$

You can watch your meal being prepared in the kitchen, including the large wood-fire oven. This Little Italy favorite will not disappoint. Especially good are the grilled fish and pork dishes. Plenty of vegetarian options. *Info*: 2210 Kettner Blvd. Tel. 619/955-8495. Open daily at 4:30pm. www.herbandwood.com.

Cowboy Star $$$

Meat, meat, and more meat. This fine-dining restaurant in East Village features antibiotic-free meats and has its own butcher shop. The filet mignon is mouthwatering, and if you'd like you can order it tartare with a quail egg. Attentive service. *Info*: 640 10th Ave. Tel. 619/450-5880. Open daily. www.cowboystarcs.com.

Pappalecco $

Where else but Little Italy would you find great gelato? Not a large place, so grab a cone or cup and head outside to walk around. Lots of choices, from fruit flavors to hazelnut. A perfect treat to end your evening. *Info*: 1602 State St. Tel. 619/238-4590. Open Mon-Thu 7am-9:30pm, Fri 7am-10pm, Sat 7:30am-10pm, Sun 7:30am-9:30pm. www.pappalecco.com. There's another location in Hillcrest at 4650 5th Ave.

Ironside Fish & Oyster $$$

This seafood restaurant, located in a historic auction house in Little Italy, is a reminder of how important the fishing industry is to San Diego. Thinking of seafood restaurants can sometimes bring to mind tacky maritime-themed décor. Not here as this contemporary space has great outdoor dining and unique touches like a wall decorated with barracuda skulls. Delicious ceviche, a shark plate, lobster roll, and oyster raw bar are just some of the interesting selections. *Info*: 1654 India St. Tel. 619/269-3033. Open daily 11am to midnight (until 2am on weekends). www.ironsidefishandoysters.com.

Cafe Gratitude

Vegans have gratitude that this restaurant in Little Italy serves a plant-based menu. Kelp noodle pesto, coconut ceviche, and adzuki beans with vegetables are only a few of the dining options here. Good selection of organic wines. *Info*: 1980 Kettner Blvd. Tel. 619/736-5077. Open daily 8am-10pm. www.cafegratitude.com.

Mimmo's Italian Village

Step into an Italian village (or so you'll think you have) and taste some of Little Italy's best Italian fare. Open since 1973, you'll find pasta dishes, a caprese salad, and plenty of delicious traditional desserts. One of their specialties is the pasta pescatore with mussels, shrimp, and calamari served in a lemon white wine cream sauce. *Info*: 1743 India St. Tel. 619/239-3710. Open daily noon-9pm. www.mimmos.biz.

CORONADO

A great way to spend your day in San Diego is to take the ferry or drive to Coronado. The historic Hotel del Coronado is located on a long, sandy beach. Stroll in the sand, rent a cabana, watch Navy ships and sailboats, and take in the great views of the Pacific Ocean. Ferries depart from 5th Avenue/600 Convention Way and Broadway Pier (North of the USS Midway Museum). Cost: $5 each way. www.coronadoferrylanding.com.

Coronado Bridge

This magnificent bridge, completed in 1969, connects downtown to Coronado. The arch is over 200 feet tall in order to allow large ships to pass under. This is important since the island is home to a large naval base. The bridge has a sad history as it's the third deadliest in the country. Only the Golden Gate Bridge in San Francisco and the Aurora Bridge in Seattle record more suicides. *Info*: California Highway Route 75.

Hotel del Coronado $$$

This majestic Victorian hotel was built in 1888. Its location on the Pacific Ocean and the powdery white sand beach make it an incredible vacation destination. It was a favorite of visitors from Hollywood and was featured in the 1959 movie *Some Like It Hot* starring Marilyn Monroe, Tony Curtis, and Jack Lemmon. There's a grand lobby fitting for a resort that once was the largest in the world. You can sip a drink at the Sunset Bar or dine under the dome in the Crown Room ($$$). Phenomenal in every respect. *Info*: 1500 Orange Ave. Tel. 619/435-6611. www.hoteldel.com.

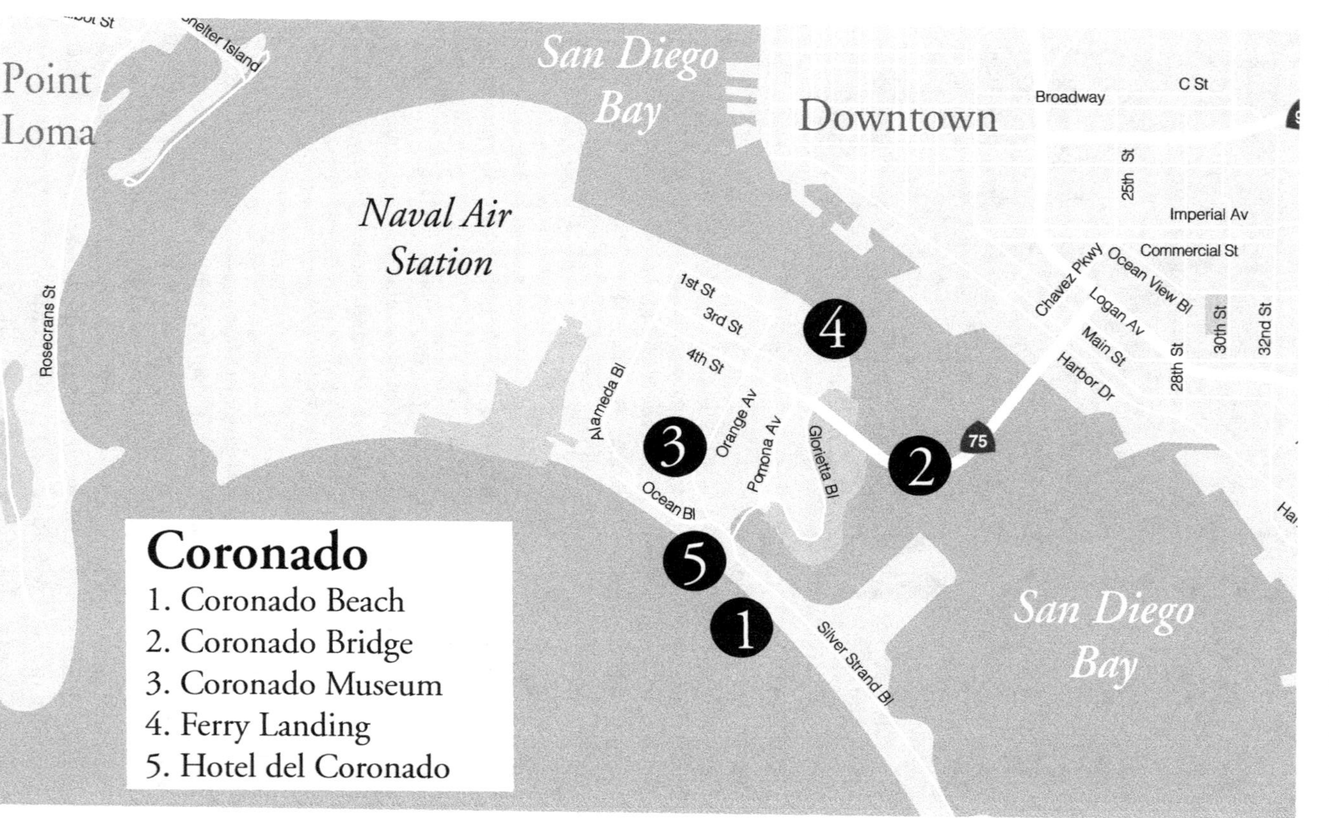
Point
Loma
Shelter Island
Rosecrans St
San Diego
Bay
Downtown
Broadway
C St
25th St
Imperial Av
Commercial St
Chavez Pkwy
Ocean View Bl
Logan Av
Main St
Harbor Dr
28th St
30th St
32nd St
Naval Air
Station
1st St
3rd St
4th St
Alameda Bl
Orange Av
Pomona Av
Glorietta Bl
Ocean Bl
Silver Strand Bl
75
San Diego
Bay
4
2
3
5
1
Coronado
1. Coronado Beach
2. Coronado Bridge
3. Coronado Museum
4. Ferry Landing
5. Hotel del Coronado

Coronado Museum of History and Art

This small museum explores not only Coronado, but also the history of the U.S. Navy's presence here. Exhibits feature the luxurious Hotel del Coronado and Tent City, a camping resort that catered to budget travelers. Photos and military artifacts make up a big part of the museum. *Info*: 1100 Orange Ave. Tel. 619/435-7242. Open daily in summer 10am-5pm (10am-4pm in winter). Admission: Free. www.coronadohistory.org.

Eating & Drinking in Coronado

In addition to the restaurants and bars at the Hotel del Coronado (*see above*), here are other suggestions for wining and dining in Coronado.

Lobster West $-$$

Seafood, seafood, and more seafood. Shrimp, scallops, and crab are on the menu. Most come here for the specialty, a delicious lobster roll. *Info*: 1033 B Ave. Tel. 619/675-0002. Open daily 11am-8pm. www.lobsterwest.com.

Coronado Brewing Company $$

A large selection of beers by the bottle and can (try the Salty Crew Blonde Ale) and good pub food at this Coronado favorite. Located at the ferry landing, it has a great view of the San Diego skyline from the outdoor patio. The menu includes pizza, burgers, tacos, and salads. *Info*: 170 Orange Ave. Tel. 619/437-4452. Open daily 11am-9pm. www.coronadobrewingcompany.com.

Leroy's Kitchen and Lounge $$$

Farm-to-table fare at this attractive restaurant with a comfortable interior featuring a large chalkboard menu and a spacious outdoor patio. Fresh ingredients, fresh seafood, and grass-fed meats. The menu changes based on the season. You'll also be able to sip a cocktail or craft beer, and choose from an interesting wine list (many of the selections are organic). *Info*: 1015 Orange Ave. Tel. 619/437-6087. Open daily 11am-10pm. bluebridgehospitality.com/leroyskitchenandlounge/.

BARRIO LOGAN

The Barrio Logan neighborhood in south central San Diego is the epicenter of Mexican-American culture. The Coronado Bridge here is painted with huge, colorful murals on its pillars, depicting the city's Mexican community. Known as Chicano Park, it's the site of the largest collection of Chicano murals in the world. If you're looking for authentic Mexican cuisine, this is the place to come. After all, San Diego is only 17 miles (27 km) from the border of Mexico. Here are a few eateries you should check out:

Panchita's Bakery

Pan dulce (pastries) are found at this traditional *panadería* with over 160 varieties of breads, pastries, cookies, and desserts. They also have excellent coffee and hot chocolate (for those rare cold days in San Diego). *Info*: 1879 Logan Ave. Tel. 619/338-9331. Open daily. panchitasbakery.com.

Las Quatros Milpas

Just wait in line and you'll be rewarded with authentic Mexican food. Tortillas are made fresh daily. For breakfast try the eggs with chorizo served with rice and beans. Delicious empanadas with all sorts of fillings, including pumpkin. *Info*: 1857 Logan Ave. Tel. 619/234-4460. Closed Sun. www.las-quatros-milpas.com.

¡Salud!

Fish tacos are great here, but you'll also want to try the barrio taco (beef, beans, and nopal cactus) and the ceviche. Authentic, delicious, and inexpensive. *Info*: 2196 Logan Ave. Tel. 619/255-3856. Closed Sun. www.saludtacos.com.

Border X Brewing

This Latin-owned brewery—the first in the city—serves Mexican craft beer. You can choose from an interesting selection of beers like Blood Saison that gets its red hue from hibiscus, the wheat beer Gran Jefe, and Abuelita's, a chocolate stout. *Info*: 2181 Logan Ave. Tel. 619/501-0503. Open daily. www.borderxbrewing.com.

OLD TOWN

This is the the oldest settled area in the city. It contains Old Town San Diego State Historic Park and Presidio Park, both of which are listed on the National Register of Historic Places. It's a bit touristy, but worth checking out for the interesting museums, souvenir shops, and restaurants. *Info*: Located 3.5 miles (5.6 km) north of Downtown at the junction of I-5 and I-8.

Whaley House Museum

Built in 1857 and decorated with period furniture, this building served as a store, theater, and courthouse. Allegedly haunted, the museum features a section on the murders and deaths that took place here when it served as the site of hangings when it was a courthouse. *Info*: 2476 San Diego Ave. Tel. 619/297-7511. Open daily Memorial Day to Labor Day. Closed Wed from Labor Day to Memorial Day. Admission: $7. Nighttime visits Thu-Sun $13. www.whaleyhouse.org.

El Campo Santo Cemetery

Speaking of haunted, San Diego's first graveyard is filled with nearly 450 graves created between 1850 and 1880. Wooden crosses and markers make for an interesting "sight" to visit. *Info*: 2410 San Diego Ave. Tel. 619/220-5422. Admission: Free. Tours through www.hiddensandiego.net.

Heritage Park Victorian Village

A must for fans of historical architecture, seven Victorian buildings were moved here from throughout the city. The brightly covered structures are just for looking at and photographing from the outside. Two places where you can tour the interiors are the city's first synagogue, Temple Beth Israel, dating back to 1889 and the Senlis Cottage, a working-class home from the 19th century. *Info*: 2454 Heritage Park Row. Tel. 858/565-3600. Open daily 9am-5pm. Admission: Free.
www.sdparks.org.

Old Town San Diego State Historic Park

In the 1800s, adobe buildings were built here to house Spanish soldiers. Some of the structures are the city's oldest. Many of the buildings now contain restaurants and shops. Among the many sights here are:

• Cosmopolitan Hotel and Restaurant, dating back to 1870.
• Mason Street School, the first public school house in San Diego.
• The adobe houses Casa de Estudillo (1827), Casa de Machado y Silvas (1840), and Casa de Machado y Stewart (1835).
• San Diego Union Museum, a mid-19th century print shop.
• Wells Fargo History Museum located in the Colorado House, with its bank vault and telegraph office.
Info: 4002 Wallace St. Tel. 858/220-5422. Open daily May-Sep 10am-5pm, Oct-Apr 10am-4pm (until 5pm on weekends). Admission: Free. www.parks.ca.gov.

Presidio Park

This lovely park was the site of the San Diego Presidio and the San Diego Mission, the first European settlements in the Western U.S. You can take in the views of Mission Bay and the Pacific Ocean. The Junípero Serra Museum here presents the history of San Diego. *Info*: 2811 Jackson St. Tel. 619/692-4918. Open daily 6am-10pm. Admission: Free. www.sandiego.gov.

4. Ocean Beach/ Point Loma

• Ocean Beach
• Cabrillo National Monument
• Sunset Cliffs Natural Park
• Fort Rosecrans National Cemetery
• Shelter Island
• Harbor Island
• Liberty Station
• Eating & Drinking in
Ocean Beach and Point Loma

OCEAN BEACH/POINT LOMA

Surfers, sunbathers, and fishers hang out at Ocean Beach. Check out the Ocean Beach Farmers Market and the main drag Newport Avenue, filled with boutiques, pubs, and antique shops. The Point Loma Peninsula is known for its seafood restaurants, especially on Shelter and Harbor islands. Liberty Station (a former Naval Training Center) has interesting shops and eateries. Also here are Sunset Cliffs Natural Park and the Cabrillo National Monument, a park with trails, tide pools, and interesting exhibits on Southern California history.

Ocean Beach

Ocean Beach (locals call it "OB") used to be a destination for fun at an amusement park that was on its beach in the early 1900s. Today it draws laid-back locals and visitors who sunbathe and surf. This small community has avoided the influx of the chain stores and restaurants that are found in other beach towns. Quirky, groovy, and diverse, this is Southern California at its finest. The pier is located at the west end of Niagara Ave and you'll find plenty of people strolling, fishing, and taking in the sunset. Extending a half mile, it's one of the longest in California and even has a cafe. In town, you'll find taco joints, swimwear stores, and souvenir shops. *Info*: Public parking is located at the foot of Voltaire St., at the foot of Santa Monica Ave., and at the foot of Newport Ave. To get here from Downtown, take I-8 west to Sunset Cliffs Blvd. and turn right on West Point Loma Blvd.

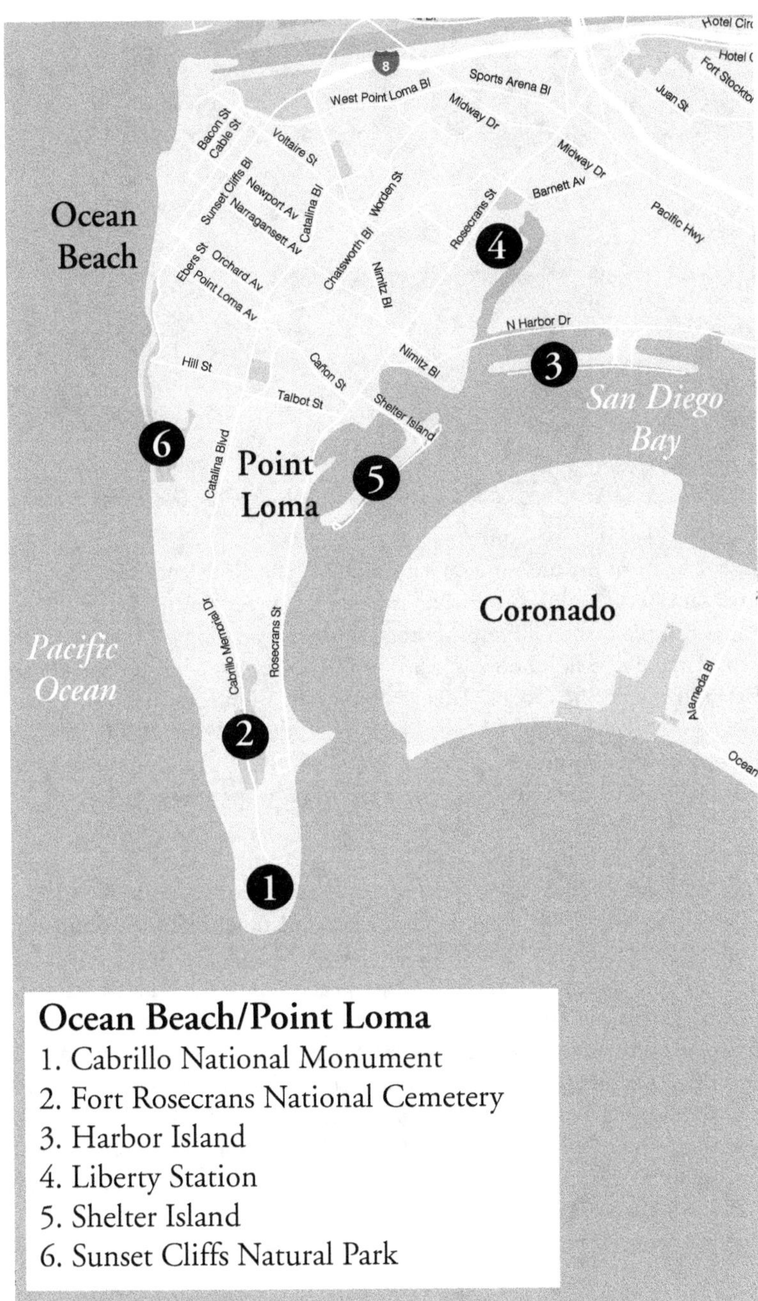

Ocean Beach/Point Loma
1. Cabrillo National Monument
2. Fort Rosecrans National Cemetery
3. Harbor Island
4. Liberty Station
5. Shelter Island
6. Sunset Cliffs Natural Park

Cabrillo National Monument

At the heart of the monument is a statue of Juan Rodríguez Cabrillo, the first European explorer to arrive in San Diego. At the highest point on the peninsula is the Old Point Loma Lighthouse, dating back to the 19th century (the new lighthouse is nearby). There are great views of San Diego Bay and the Pacific Ocean. This is a big destination for walkers and hikers, especially the scenic 2.5 mile (4 km) Bayside Trail. *Info*: 1800 Cabrillo Memorial Dr. (Point Loma). Tel. 619/557-5450. Open daily 9am-5pm. Admission: $15 per vehicle, $7 per walker. www.nps.gov/cabr.

Sunset Cliffs Natural Park

Incredible views from this 68-acre park located along the Pacific Ocean in Ocean Beach. Walk along the dramatic sandstone cliffs and admire the impressive homes on Sunset Cliffs Boulevard. In addition to the expansive ocean views, there's an intertidal area and acres of restored native habitat. This is a popular setting for those wanting to take in the surfers and incredibly colorful sunsets. The park is also a haven for walkers and hikers and there are plenty of trails. We'd be remiss if we didn't warn you that you should stay away from the edge of the cliffs, as they can be unstable and dangerous. *Info*: 1300 Sunset Cliffs Blvd./South of Ladera St. Open sunrise to sunset. Admission: Free. www.sunsetcliffs.info. There's a large parking lot at the southern end.

Fort Rosecrans National Cemetery

This military cemetery is a final resting place for fallen soldiers. The views from its 78 acres include the bay, ocean, and city skyline. Those buried here include casualties of the Battle of San Pasqual of the Mexican-American War in 1846 through World War II. There are many memorials here including The Patriots of America Memorial dedicated to all Americans who answered the call to arms. *Info*: 1800 Cabrillo Memorial Dr (Point Loma). Tel. 858/658-7360. Open sunrise to sunset. Admission: Free. www.cem. va.gov/CEMs/nchp/ftrosecrans.asp.

Liberty Station

What a great example of repurposing space. This former naval training center has been turned into a commercial arts district. Over 100 acres that used to be home to military structures now have restaurants, shopping, and boutiques featuring local artists. Also here are a golf course, seasonal ice-skating rink (yes, you heard that right), cinemas, and a public market (*see below*). On the first Friday of each month, an art festival features galleries, dance performances, and music. And, it's all free. *Info*: The area around Barnett Ave., North Harbor Dr., Chauncery Rd., and Rosecrans St. (Point Loma). www.libertystation.com.

Shelter Island

This lovely "island" (it's connected to the mainland by a strip of land) has one street, Shelter Island Drive. The peninsula is only 1.2 miles (2 km) long. It's home to hotels and restaurants serving fresh seafood. The attractive marina features spectacular yachts and sailboats. *Info*: Southeast of Rosecrans St. (Point Loma).

Harbor Island

Like Shelter Island, this attractive spot is not an island, but a peninsula. It's home to hundreds of pleasure craft, a few restaurants, and hotels. A popular departure point for boat charters. Great views of the city skyline and planes taking off and landing at the airport just north of here. *Info*: South of North Harbor Dr. (Point Loma).

Eating & Drinking in Ocean Beach and Point Loma

Ocean Beach Pier Cafe $-$$

Park near the beach and start walking on the long pier. Near the end, you'll reach this unique place to eat breakfast, lunch, and dinner. Some of the options include lobster quesadillas, lobster tacos, mahi-mahi tacos, and clam chowder.

Although seafood is the focus here, they also serve burgers, hot dogs, grilled cheese, and salads. The "Captain's Platter" has shrimp, pollack, and halibut. Great views! *Info*: 5091 Niagara Ave. Tel. 619/226-3474. Open daily 8am-10pm. No reservations. No credit cards. No toilet facilities, but there are public restrooms on the pier.

Liberty Public Market $-$$$

There's something for everyone at this public market in Point Loma. Browse more than 30 food, beverage, and artisan vendors selling beer, wine, cocktails, produce, fish, pastas, and desserts. Some of your choices include:
• Le Parfait Paris: French patisserie and boulangerie
• Local Greens: Salads, wraps, and bowls
• Landini's Pizzeria: New York style pizza by the slice
• Cecilia's Taqueria: Mexican dining
• Latin Chef: Peruvian cuisine
• Pasta Design: Handcrafted pastas
• The Pig's Gig: Texas style BBQ
• Stone World Bistro & Garden: Farm-to-table restaurant and craft brewery

Info: 2820 Decatur Rd. Open daily 11am-7pm. bluebridgehospitality.com/libertypublicmarket/

Hodad's $

At this Ocean Beach burger joint, you'll likely wait in line to taste the large, juicy patties. Delicious fries and thick milkshakes add to the appeal. The fun and funky decor features walls covered with personalized license plates. And you might even be dining in a vintage Volkswagen van. *Info*: 5010 Newport Ave. Tel. 619/224-4623. Open daily 11am-10pm. There are also a locations at Petco Park during events and downtown at 945 Broadway. Tel. 619/234-6323. Open daily 11am-9pm. www.hodadies.com.

OB Noodle House $$

Just a block from the Ocean Beach pier, this popular restaurant serves Asian food. Lots of vegetarian, vegan, and gluten-free options. Try the Korean beef short ribs or the Sizzling Fish (freshwater Vietnamese Basa). *Info*: 4993 Niagara Ave. (Ocean Beach). Tel. 619/255-9858. Open daily Mon-Thu noon-11pm, Fri-Sun 11am-11pm. www.obnoodlehouse.com.

Point Loma Seafoods $$

It's all about the freshness of the fish at this deli counter. Sushi, fish tacos, cod, ceviche, and seafood salads are on the menu here. Add fries and coleslaw and you've got a delicious meal. *Info*: 2805 Emerson St. (Shelter Island). Tel 619/223-1109. Open daily 9am-8pm. www.pointlomaseafoods.com.

WHALE WATCHING

The "peaceful giants of the sea" come to the warm lagoons in the Gulf of California to breed. The whales come within miles of San Diego's coastline and can be viewed on daily whale watching excursions and from Cabrillo National Monument on Point Loma. Whale watching tours begin at $50 and can be booked through www.sdwhalewatch.com and www.adventureribrides.com.

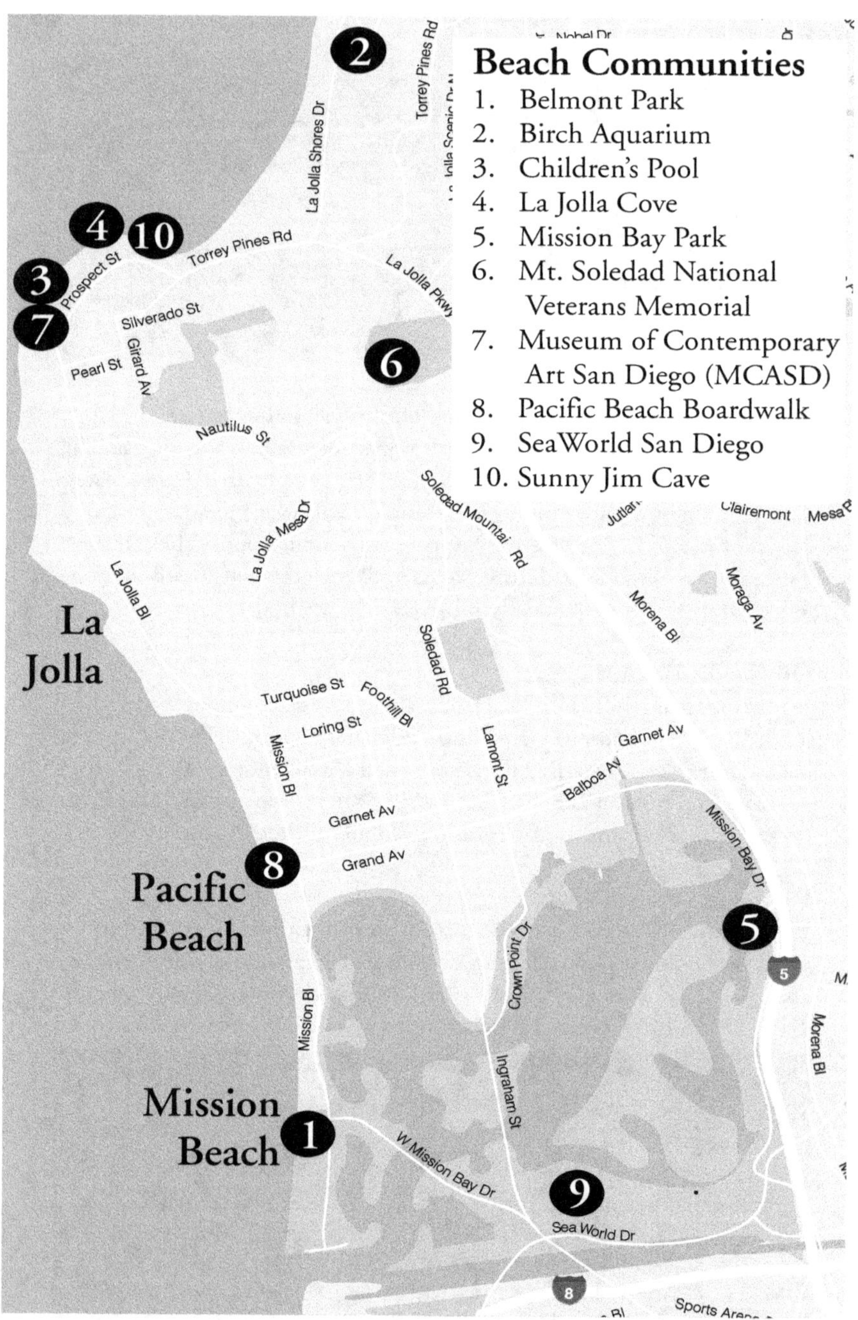

Beach Communities

1. Belmont Park
2. Birch Aquarium
3. Children's Pool
4. La Jolla Cove
5. Mission Bay Park
6. Mt. Soledad National Veterans Memorial
7. Museum of Contemporary Art San Diego (MCASD)
8. Pacific Beach Boardwalk
9. SeaWorld San Diego
10. Sunny Jim Cave

5. Beach Communities

- Mission Bay Park
- Belmont Park
- Pacific Beach Boardwalk
- SeaWorld San Diego
- Eating & Drinking in Mission Bay and Pacific Beach
- La Jolla
- Museum of Contemporary Art San Diego (MCASD)
- Birch Aquarium
- Children's Pool
- La Jolla Cove
- Sunny Jim Cave
- Mt. Soledad National Veterans Memorial
- Eating & Drinking in La Jolla
- Torrey Pines State Natural Reserve/ Black's Beach

MISSION BEACH AND PACIFIC BEACH

One of the main reasons that San Diego is such a popular travel destination is its fantastic beaches. With glorious weather most of the year, visitors are likely to spend some time hanging out at the beach. Mission Bay is home to Belmont Park, an amusement park complete with rollercoaster and surfing demonstrations. Also here is the extremely popular SeaWorld San Diego. Just north of Mission Bay is Pacific Beach, where you can enjoy surfing and sunbathing. It's known for its fun vibe and there are plenty of bars and restaurants that attract a young, vibrant crowd.

Mission Bay Park

This artificial bay is a popular destination for watersports. You'll find everything from kayaks to sailboats to jet skis. If you're not in the mood to get wet, hang out on one of the many beaches here or take a walk or bike ride on the path that circles the bay. *Info*: 2688 E. Mission Bay Dr.

Belmont Park

On Mission Beach (on the east side of the bay) is this amusement park. You'll find the usual roller coaster, arcade, carousel, and bumper cars here. There's also a zip line, rock-climbing wall, laser tag, and plenty of places to eat. *Info*: 3146 Mission Blvd. Tel. 858/228-9283. Open daily 11am-8pm (until 10pm on Fri and Sat). Admission and parking are free, but each ride charges a fee. Online passes for all attractions is $30. www.belmontpark.com.

SeaWorld San Diego

This aquatic park, located on the south end of Mission Bay, has thousands of mammals and creatures of the sea. Its most popular shows include Dolphin Days, Sea Lions Live, and the famous Orca Encounter. It was this last show that has been the subject of controversy and demonstrations by animal rights activists. In the show, black-and-white killer whales jump out of the water and splash spectators when their four-ton bodies hit the water. After a documentary *Blackfish* looked into training and living conditions of the whales, SeaWorld was forced to review its mission. In response SeaWorld has moved to improve its habitats and announced that it would phase out killer whale shows after the orcas living here have died. This combination aquarium, zoo, and showplace continues to be highly popular. *Info*: 500 Sea World Dr. Tel. 619/222-4732. Open daily 10am-5pm (until 9pm in summer and winter holidays). Admission: $93.99, under 10 free. www.seaworld.com.

Pacific Beach Boardwalk
(Ocean Front Walk)

Pacific Beach ("PB") is the ultimate in people watching. The boardwalk begins at the end of Mission Beach and passes the Crystal Pier and Pacific Beach Park. The crowd skews young and fun. Beachfront restaurants and bars overlook the water. Speaking of looking, there is plenty of "eye candy" to keep you busy. *Info*: Between Pacific Beach Dr. and Garnet Ave. (Pacific Beach).

Eating & Drinking in Mission Beach and Pacific Beach
Sushi Ota $$$
Chef and owner Yukito Ota is known for his inventive takes on sushi, sashimi, and seafood dishes. Nothing really fancy about the dining area, but you'll be thinking about the food anyway. Don't forget to order the specialty here, local sea urchin (uni). There's usually a wait, so reservations are recommended. *Info*: 4529 Mission Bay Dr. (Pacific Beach). Tel. 858/270-5670. Open daily for dinner. Lunch Tue-Fri. www.sushiota.com.

Oscars $
Oscars, which has several locations throughout San Diego, is known for their fish tacos. It's not all about the fish tacos here as you can order fish stew, ceviche, and steak tacos, too. If you're here for breakfast, make sure you order the hearty breakfast burrito with smoked fish, bacon, ham, steak, or chorizo. *Info*: 703 Turquoise St. (North Pacific Beach). Tel. 858/488-6392. Open daily. There's another location in Pacific Beach at 746 Emerald St. Tel. 858/412-4009. www.oscarsmexicanseafood.com.

Sandbar Sports Grill $$
This fun, casual eatery is located on the boardwalk north of the Belmont Park amusement park in Mission Beach. Everything from burgers to salads to sandwiches. Especially popular are the large nacho plates. Lots of choices of beer by the glass. Not fine dining, but the setting and people-watching are excellent. *Info*: 718 Ventura Pl. (Mission Beach). Tel. 858/488-1274. Open daily. www.sandbarsportsgrill.com.

The Fishery $$$

Fish, fish, and more fish. There's no meat or chicken on the menu, rather the chef focuses on local fresh seafood. You can order your seafood pan-roasted, grilled, or braised. The garlicky shrimp scampi is delicious. *Info*: 5040 Cass St. (Pacific Beach). *Info*: 858/272-9985. Open daily. www.the-fishery.com.

Pacific Beach Fish Shop $$

Just look for the large marlin trophy on the front of this casual fish shop. Sandwiches, grilled fish, tacos, and ceviche are just some of the offerings. Head outside to the patio to enjoy your fresh fish. You can order your dish by type of fish, marinade, and style (taco, salad, plate, or sandwich), which makes for tons of dining options. *Info*: 1775 Garnet Ave. (Pacific Beach). Tel. 858/483-4746. Open daily. www.thefishshoppb.com.

Saska's $$-$$$

If you're tired of all that seafood, head to Mission Beach's original steak-house. Opened in the early 1950s, but renovated since then, it's your classic steakhouse. Prime rib is a specialty, but you'll also have familiar dishes like wedge salads, shrimp cocktail, and Alaskan king crab. *Info*: 3768 Mission Blvd. (Mission Beach). Tel 858/488-7311. Open daily for dinner. www.saskas.com.

LA JOLLA

The famous shoreline of the picturesque village of La Jolla keeps travelers returning again and again. This luxurious town, north of Pacific Beach, provides oceanside serenity and many options for dining, sleeping, and shopping. There are plenty of sights here, from a contemporary art museum to lovely coves. *Info*: From Downtown San Diego 14 miles (22.5 km). www.lajollabythesea.com.

Birch Aquarium

This aquarium, operated by the Scripps Institution of Oceanography and the University of California San Diego, reminds us of the importance of the ocean to San Diego over the years. Interactive exhibits are designed to encourage kids to learn more about aquatic life. The feeding shows are the most popular as you can watch sharks eyeing their food and lobsters appearing from nowhere to feed. A deck with incredible views of La Jolla provides access to touchable tide pools. *Info*: 2300 Expedition Way. Tel. 858/534-3474. Open daily 9am-5pm. Admission: $19.50, ages 3-17 $15, age 60 plus $16.50, students $16, under 3 free. www.aquarium.ucsd.edu.

Museum of Contemporary Art San Diego (MCASD)

The main branch of this museum, located in a fantastic location in La Jolla, is currently closed for renovation and expansion. There are nearly 5,000 pieces of post-World War II art in the museum's collection. Some of the collection and exhibits are shown at the Downtown location. Among the art are works by Christo (*Wrapped Package*), Ellsworth Kelly (*Red, Blue, Green*), and Franz Kline (*Untitled, 1953, black and white gouache on paper*). *Info*: 700 Prospect St. Tel. 858/454-3541. www.mcasd.org.

Children's Pool

This small beach got its name after a breakwater was constructed by local philanthropist Ellen Browning Scripps in 1931. She wanted to create a safe place for local children to swim and play. Today, you can't swim in the waters as the area has been taken over by sea lions. People come here to watch them and their pups frolic on the rocks and in the water. *Info*: 850 Coast Blvd. (La Jolla).

Sunny Jim's Sea Cave

Tours (about 20 minutes long) guide you through the century-old tunnel. Gustav Schultz, a German engineer, hired Chinese laborers to dig the tunnel to facilitate smuggling immigrants and later liquor and opium during Prohibition. Schultz's residence, now the Cave Store, leads to 144 stairs into the cave and tunnel. At the Cave Store, you can purchase souvenirs and rent snorkeling gear and paddleboards. This is just one of several smuggler's caves in La Jolla. *Info*: 1325 Coast Blvd. (La Jolla). Tel. 858/459-0746. Open daily 9am-5pm. Admission: $10, $7 ages 3-17. Reservations through www.cavestore.com.

La Jolla Cove

Surrounded by cliffs, this picturesque beach and cove is a huge destination for scuba divers and snorkelers. Rich with marine life, it's also home to sea lions that swim here and bask in the sun on the large rocks of the cove. You can swim here on the small beach, but there are large swells in the winter that make it difficult for beach dwellers, yet great for surfers. *Info*: 1100 Coast Blvd. (La Jolla).

Mt. Soledad National Veterans Memorial

Located at the highest point in La Jolla, this memorial to veterans has panoramic views of the countryside and ocean. Black granite plaques honor veterans with a description of their service. Its focal point is a 29-foot cross. There's a large memorial devoted to veterans of the Korean War. *Info*: 6905 La Jolla Scenic Dr. Tel. 858/459-2314. Open daily 7am-10pm. Admission: Free. www.soledadmemorial.com.

Eating & Drinking in La Jolla

Catania $$-$$$

This Italian restaurant, with a lovely deck, serves handmade pasta dishes like butternut squash ravioli and squid ink linguine. There are many options for a wood fire pizza. Main dishes include branzino and wood-grilled rib eye. Interesting Italian wine list. *Info*: 7863 Girard Ave. (Third Floor). Tel. 858/551-5105. Open daily for lunch and dinner. www.cataniasd.com.

Nine-Ten $$$

Located in the Grand Colonial Hotel, this award-winning restaurant serves innovative California cuisine. If you request terrace dining, you'll have a sunset view of the Pacific Ocean. Dinner selections include roasted Liberty Farms duck breast and Mexican broomtail grouper. Delicious Nine-Ten burger. Good wine list that's heavy on California selections. *Info*: 910 Prospect St. Tel. 858/964-5400. Reservations recommended. www.nine-ten.com.

Burger Lounge $

Dining can be pricey in La Jolla Village, so try this local chain that offers grass-fed burgers, organic quinoa veggie burgers, and free-range turkey burgers. Excellent fries and onion rings. Beer and wine are also available. *Info*: 1101 Wall St. Tel. 858/456-0196. Open daily for lunch and dinner. www.burgerlounge.com.

Marine Room $$$

On the water in La Jolla Shores, so close that waves splash against the windows, this local staple has been here since the 1940s. Don't expect California contemporary cuisine as you'll be dining on such classics as rack of lamb provençal and lobster tail. Large international wine list. *Info*: 2000 Spindrift Dr. Tel. 858/459-7222. Dinner only. Reservations recommended. www.marineroom.com.

The Taco Stand $

There just might be a line out the door at this popular Mexican restaurant. It's inspired by the taco stands of Tijuana and features not only tacos (with handmade corn tortillas), but also quesadillas, burritos, and carne asada fries. Down it all with a cold Mexican beer. *Info*: 621 Pearl St. Tel. 858/551-6666. Open daily for breakfast, lunch, and dinner. www.letstaco.com.

El Pescador Fish Market $-$$

A La Jolla institution, this deli, market, and restaurant in La Jolla Village is known for its glass counter filled with fresh fish. Try the El Pescador (crab, shrimp, and smoked salmon) served as either a sandwich or salad. *Info*: 634 Pearl St. Tel. 858/456-2526. Open daily 11am-9pm. www.elpescadorfishmarket.com.

TORREY PINES STATE NATURAL PARK/BLACK'S BEACH

Our favorite park in the area, the scenic 300-foot cliffs make for the perfect get away from the bustle of the city. For many, the highlight is the two-mile-long Black's Beach. You can reach it down (and up!) a steep path from the gliderport (*see below*). Not for the unfit. You'll be rewarded with a long, sandy beach and chill vibe once you reach the ocean beach. A portion of the beach is considered clothing-optional and the far north end is popular with the LGBTQ community.

Black's Beach is located just north of La Jolla Shores and beneath the Torrey Pines bluffs. It gets its name from the Black family, who owned a horse farm on the cliffs overlooking the beach. There are two sections. The southern section is owned by the city of San Diego and the northern section is owned by the State of California. Black's Beach is a popular destination for surfers as it has one of the strongest surf breaks in Southern California. An underwater canyon, Scripps Canyon, funnels waves toward the shore. Only recommended for experienced surfers.

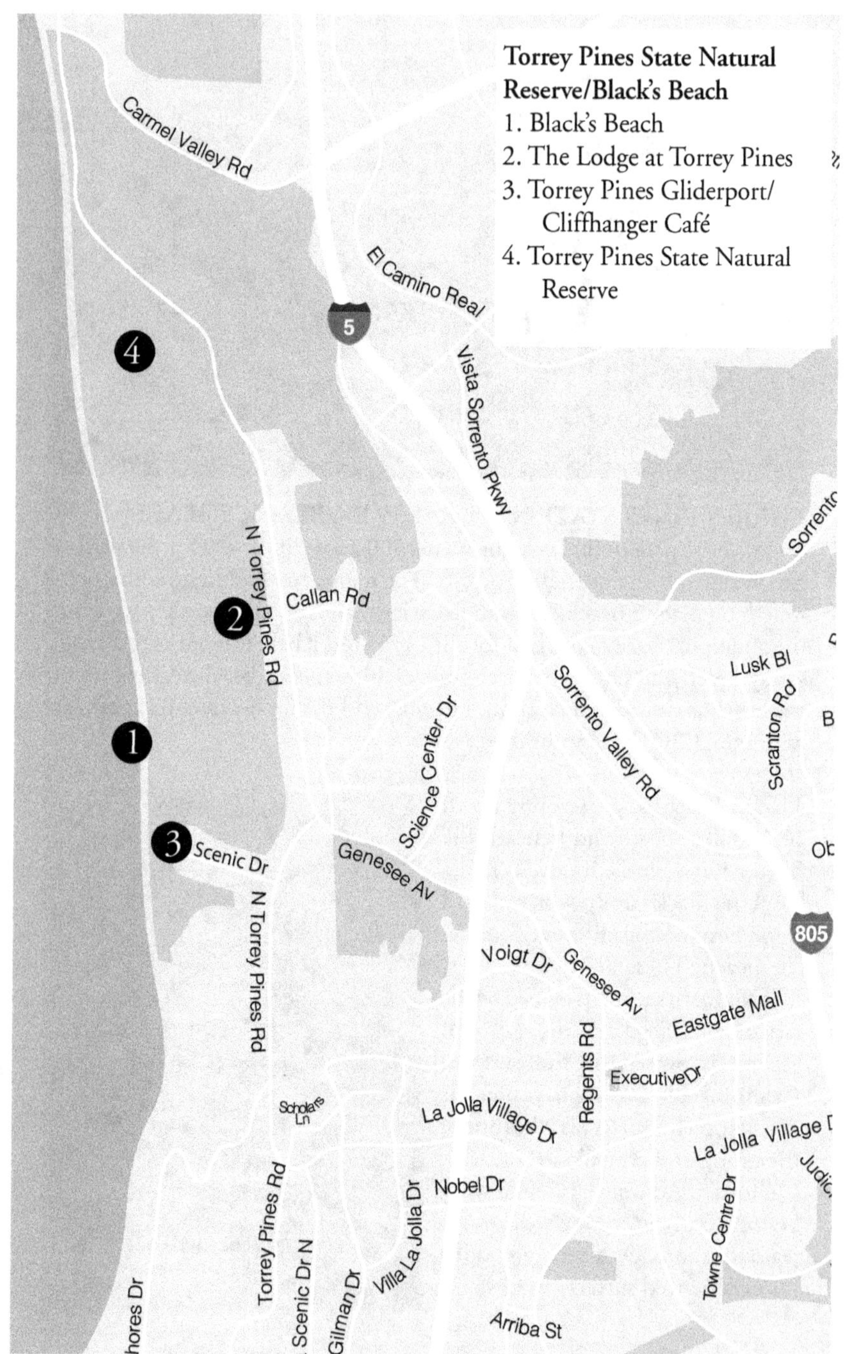
Torrey Pines State Natural
Reserve/Black's Beach
1. Black's Beach
2. The Lodge at Torrey Pines
3. Torrey Pines Gliderport/
   Cliffhanger Café
4. Torrey Pines State Natural
   Reserve
Carmel Valley Rd
El Camino Real
5
Vista Sorrento Pkwy
Sorrento
N Torrey Pines Rd
Callan Rd
Lusk Bl
Scranton Rd
B
Science Center Dr
Sorrento Valley Rd
Scenic Dr
Genesee Av
Ob
N Torrey Pines Rd
Voigt Dr
Genesee Av
805
Eastgate Mall
Regents Rd
Executive Dr
Scholars Ln
La Jolla Village Dr
La Jolla Village D
Torrey Pines Rd
Scenic Dr N
Gilman Dr
Villa La Jolla Dr
Nobel Dr
Towne Centre Dr
Judi
hores Dr
Arriba St

The **Torrey Pines Gliderport** sits above the cliffs. If you're not as chicken as the writers of this book, you can hang glide with an experienced pilot along the ocean and cliffs. *Info*: 2800 Torrey Pines Scenic Dr. Open daily (weather permitting). Cost from $175. www.flytorrey.com. Even if you're not interested in going airborne, you can sit back and watch others at the **Cliffhanger Café**. You'll have great views of the gliderport and the Pacific Ocean. Paragliders and hang gliders launch right in front of the outdoor patio. The cafe offers sandwiches, salads, snacks, and soup.

Info: 2800 Torrey Pines Scenic Drive. Tel. 858/452-9858. Open daily 9am to 4pm. www.flytorrey.com.

If you're interested in more upscale dining, you can visit nearby **The Lodge at Torrey Pines**, where you'll find the elegant **A.R. Valentien** ($$$) with breathtaking views of the Torrey Pines Golf Course and the Pacific Ocean from its patio. For more moderately priced fare, **The Grill** ($$) features wood-fired dishes and local craft beers. It also has an outdoor patio with great views. *Info*: 11480 N. Torrey Pines Rd. (La Jolla). Tel. 858/777-6641 (restaurant), 858/777-6635 (grill). Open daily. www.thelodgetorreypines.com.

Info: There are several ways to reach the beach. The most commonly used access point is the Torrey Pines Gliderport Trail, which departs from the Gliderport. Remember, you are descending over 300 feet to the beach (and then have to return the same way)! Other points of access are the Torrey Pines State Park entrance, the Torrey Pines State Beach, and from La Jolla Shores (which can be blocked at high tide).

The easiest way to arrive at Black's Beach from downtown San Diego is via I-5. Take exit 29 onto Genesee Avenue, left on Genesee Ave., left onto N. Torrey Pines Rd., and right onto Torrey Pines Scenic Dr. There is ample parking here. The beach is located 15 miles (24 km) from Downtown San Diego.

6. Inland Neighborhoods

- Hillcrest
- University Heights
- Normal Heights
- North Park
- South Park/ Golden Hill
- La Jolla
- Mission Hills
- LGBTQ Bars and Nighlife
- Eating & Drinking

INLAND NEIGHBORHOODS

San Diego is filled with diverse and interesting neighborhoods. We'll explore some of the lively neighborhoods in the city. From the center of LGBTQ life in Hillcrest to the fun fairs in Normal Heights, there's something for every visitor.

Hillcrest

This fun and vibrant neighborhood is located north of Downtown and Balboa Park. It's the center of life for the city's large LGBTQ community, but you don't have to identify as such in order to enjoy its many offerings.

The east end of the neighborhood is marked by an enormous rainbow flag just off University Avenue near Normal Street. Ethnically diverse restaurants, home decor stores, boutiques, bars, nightclubs, wine bars, and craft breweries line the streets. You'll also find a large farmers market here (*see below*).

Farmers Market

Every Sunday, this market features everything from gourmet food, produce, beer, and coffee to arts and crafts. *Info*: Intersection of Normal St. and Lincoln Ave. Sundays from 9am-2pm.

At Fifth Avenue and University Avenue, you'll see the large neon "Hillcrest" sign spanning the street. In addition to LGBTQ bars, you can also get lost exploring the interesting vintage clothing shops, bookstores, Landmark Cinemas (featuring the latest independent and foreign films), and eateries for every budget and taste. You might enjoy strolling through the neighborhood and checking out the Craftsman and Spanish-style homes.

Linda Vista Rd
Morena
Friars Rd
Fashion Valley Rd
Frazee
Cam
Hotel Circle North
Uni
He
Old
Town
Hotel Circle South
Fort Stockton Dr
Lewis St
na Bl
Juan St
Front St
Arbor Dr
Mission
Hills
Washington St
Goldfinch St
Hillcrest
Midway Dr
Barnett Av
5
163
Pacific Hwy
Reynard Wy
1st Av
4th Av
5th Av
Laurel St
arbor Dr
San Diego
Bay
Downtown

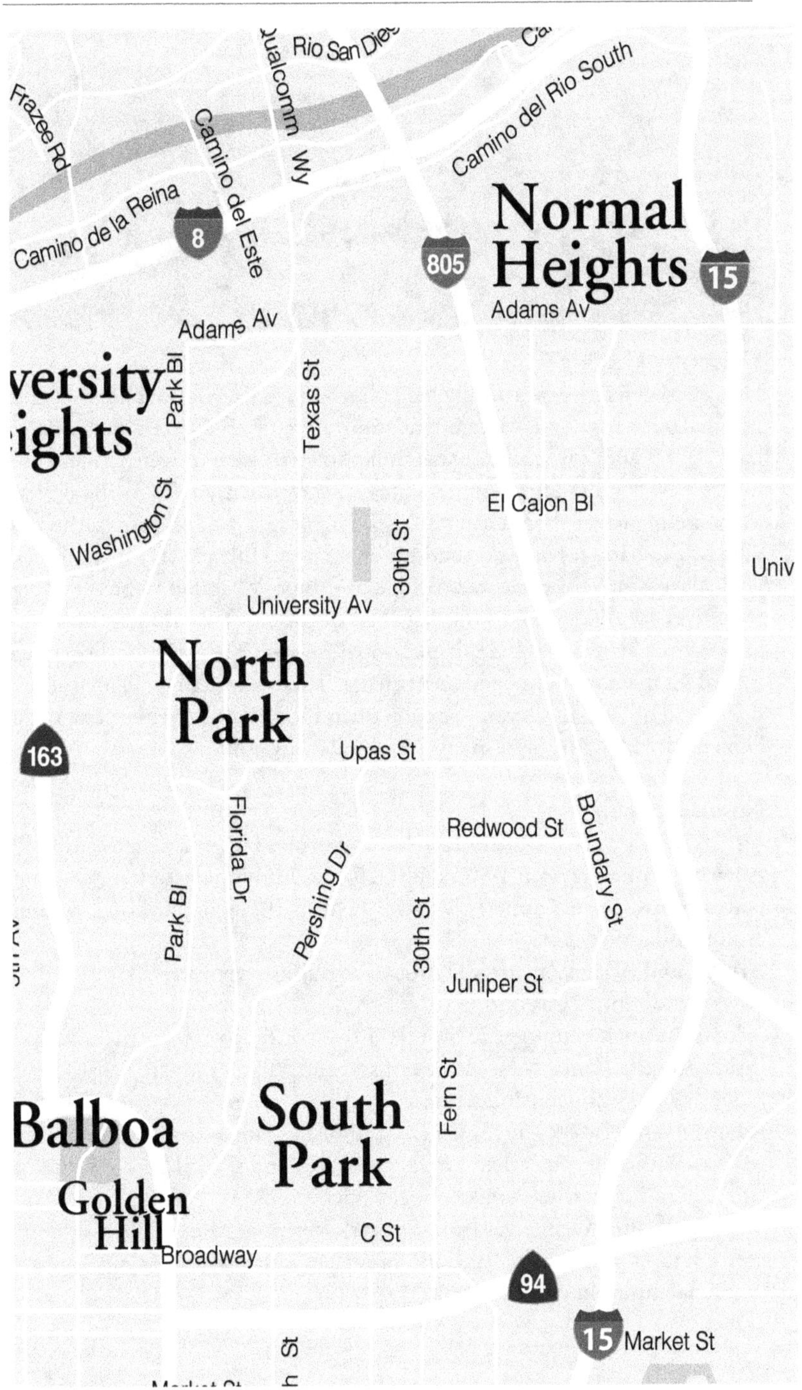
Frazee Rd
Rio San Dieg
Qualcomm Wy
Camino del Rio South
Ca
Camino de la Reina
Camino del Este
8
Normal
Heights
805
15
Adams Av
Adams Av
University
Heights
Park Bl
Texas St
Washington St
El Cajon Bl
30th St
Univ
University Av
North
Park
163
Upas St
Florida Dr
Redwood St
Boundary St
Pershing Dr
Park Bl
30th St
Juniper St
Fern St
Balboa
South
Park
Golden
Hill
C St
Broadway
94
15
Market St
Market St

University Heights

University Heights is a lovely neighborhood adjacent to Hillcrest and Normal Heights. Like Hillcrest, it's quite gay friendly. The name dates back to the 1880s when there was a plan to establish a university here, but it was never built. This is a great area to stay when you're in the city as there are plenty of short-term rentals available and you're close to the fun vibe of the bars, restaurants, and nightclubs in Hillcrest. It's just a quick walk along the Vermont Street Bridge over busy Washington Street to get to University Avenue and Hillcrest. The designers of this blue bridge created 32 panels that include inspirational quotes. The neighborhood is a mix of Craftsman homes and apartments. There's a small retail area at the north end of Park Boulevard where it turns into Adams Avenue. The neon "University Heights" sign spans Park Boulevard.

Normal Heights

Just to the east of University Heights is Normal Heights (located around Adams Avenue between I-805 and I-15), with unique eateries, bars, and coffee shops. Several fun festivals are held in the neighborhood on and around Adams Avenue:

Art Around Adams, an art and music festival in early June (www.artaroundadams.org)

Adams Avenue Unplugged, over 100 live musical performances staged inside 30 restaurants, bars, coffee houses, and galleries in late April (www. adamsavenuebusiness.com)

Adams Avenue Street Fair, Southern California's largest free two-day music festival, with 100 musical acts on seven stages and several beer gardens in late September (www. adamsavenuebusiness.com)

Taste of Adams Avenue, gastronomic trek featuring nearly 50 restaurants, coffee houses, pubs, wine bars, and breweries in late June (www. adamsavenuebusiness.com)

North Park

Located north of Balboa Park and east of Hillcrest, this hip neighborhood offers a mixture of residential and urban areas. Its center is 30th Street and University Avenue, where you'll find fun restaurants, thrift shops, brunch spots, craft beer bars, and taquerias. *Info*: www.explorenorthpark.com.

Farmers' Market

Everything from organic fruits and vegetables to handcrafted Mexican salsas at North Park's Thursday night market. *Info*: Between 29th and Ray St. on North Park Way. *Info*: Every Thursday from 3pm-7:30pm. www.northparkfarmersmarket.com.

North Park Theatre

Opened in 1929, this historic theater has hosted concerts, films, plays, and musicals featuring such diverse acts as k.d. Lang, Red Hot Chili Peppers, and Joan Rivers. **West Coast Tavern** ($$) is located in the lobby of the theater and serves food, craft beer, and handcrafted cocktails. Popular brunch on Saturdays and Sundays known for their pancake tacos and bottomless rosé and mimosas. *Info*: Theater: 2891 University Ave. Tel. 619/239-8836. www. observatorysd.com. Tavern: 619/295-1688. www.westcoasttavern.com.

South Park/Golden Hill

South Park is nestled just south of North Park. Quieter than North Park, it also has plenty of Craftsman homes. The commercial area is located mainly on 30th Street and Fern Street, and has boutiques, cafes, and bars. The South Park Walkabout is a quarterly fun-filled evening festival that showcases businesses along Fern Street. Shops and restaurants host live music and food and drink. Peaceful Golden Hill is located just south of Balboa Park.

Mission Hills

This is one of the city's oldest neighborhoods. It's located west of Hillcrest and overlooks Presidio Park and Mission Valley. Developed in the early 1900s, there are over 300 historic homes here, especially Craftsman bungalows and Spanish Revival (with a few modern mansions). If you're interested in architecture, stroll through the area north of West Washington Street.

Although most of the action is in nearby Hillcrest, Mission Hills does have a business district located along West Washington Street and Goldfinch Street.

If you're interested in plants, check out the **Mission Hills Nursery**, which has been in business since 1910 (1525 Fort Stockton Dr. Tel. 619/295-2808. Open daily 8am-5pm).

Eating & Drinking in the Inland Neighborhoods
La Bonne Table $$
In the heart of Hillcrest, this comfortable bistro with a small outdoor patio is a favorite for French food. Classic French cuisine like French onion soup and cassoulet. Try the delicious cote de porc forestiere (bone-in pork chop with a mushroom cream sauce). Lovely setting, friendly service, good French wine and beer selection. Bon appetit! *Info*: 3696 Fifth Ave. (at Pennsylvania). Tel. 619/260-8039. Open daily for dinner. Also open for Sunday brunch. labonnetablesd.net.

Farmer's Bottega $$
This farm-to-table restaurant located in the heart of Mission Hills has an eclectic decor and menu. Some of the choices include flat breads, lamb shank, stuffed quail, wild boar sausage risotto, and oxtail ravioli. Good selection of wine by the glass and bottle and a selection of craft local beers. *Info*: 860 West Washington St. Tel. 619/458-9929. Open daily for breakfast, lunch, and dinner.

LGBTQ BARS AND NIGHTLIFE

The "Gayborhood" of Hillcrest is centered along University Avenue between Second Avenue and Park Boulevard.

University Avenue (Hillcrest)

Urban MO's Bar & Grill

Festive outdoor patio, good bar food (especially juicy burgers), and a dance floor. *Info*: 308 University Ave. Tel. 619/491-0400. Open daily. urbanmos.com.

Flicks

Music videos, televised sports, dance floor, strong drinks, and go-go dancers make this a spirited place to hang out. Lots of special events, from underwear contests to karaoke. *Info*: 1017 University Ave. Tel. 619/297-2056. Open daily. sdflicks.com.

Rich's

Large and popular dance club with two bars and dance floors. On weekends, expect to wait in line to get in! *Info*: 1051 University Ave. Tel. 619/578-9349. Closed Mon and Tue. www.richssandiego.com.

Gossip Grill

You don't have to be a lady who likes ladies to enjoy this super-fun bar and grill. Lots of open-air dining and a dance floor. Drinks include Pussy Punch and Beaver Fever (those are on the Liq Her menu) and you can't go wrong ordering the LGBT (lettuce, guacamole, bacon, and tomato) sandwich. They have an "Eat Your Vaggies" part of the menu for vegetarians. *Info*: 1220 University Ave. Tel 619/260-8023. Closed Mon. gossipgrill.com.

Uptown Tavern

Stylish and friendly bar serving craft cocktails and microbrews. Dining options include a veggie mac and cheese, chicken and waffles, and flatbreads. *Info*: 1236 University Ave. Tel. 619/241-2470. Closed Mon. uptowntavernsd.com.

The Alibi

Small dive bar with pool table, small patio, stiff drinks, and juke box with fun and eclectic music. *Info*: 1403 University Ave. Tel. 619/295-0881. Open daily.

Baja Betty's

This restaurant/bar is fun, loud, and colorful. There's a large menu of tequilas and margaritas. The Mexican fare here includes burritos, spicy fajitas, and, of course, tacos. It's even more fun when there's a drag show going on! *Info*: 1421 University Ave. Tel. 619/269-8510. Open daily. bajabettyssd.com.

Hillcrest Brewing Company

Touting itself as the country's first gay-owned brewery, it's a fun place to try a stone-fired pizza, wings, or a chopped salad. A great selection of craft beers. Communal tables make for a convivial spot. *Info*: 1458 University Ave. Tel. 619/269-4323. Closed Mon. hillcrestbrewing.com.

insideOUT

Stylish restaurant and lounge with craft cocktails and upscale dining. Try the sizzling jumbo shrimp or the burgundy braised beef short ribs. *Info*: 1642 University Ave. Tel. 619/888-8623. Closed Mon. insideoutsd.com.

Fourth Avenue (Hillcrest)
Club San Diego

Feeling frisky? Make a friend for an hour or a lifetime at this male only sauna. *Info*: 3955 Fourth Ave. Tel. 619/295-0850. Closed Mon and Tue. clubsandiego.com.

Fifth Avenue (Hillcrest)
The Loft
Enjoy a strong drink at this longtime San Diego fixture. Fun theme nights like 1980s sing along on Thursdays and Hawaiian drinks on Aloha Tuesday. *Info*: 3610 5th Ave. Tel. 619/296-6407. Open daily. www.theloftbarsandiego.com.

The Rail
The city's oldest gay bar got a facelift (how appropriate for Southern California!) and continues to be a fun destination. Don't miss Latin Night on Saturday, featuring great Latin music and dancing. *Info*: 3796 5th Ave. Tel. 619/298-2233. thebrassrail.com.

Number One Fifth Avenue
This friendly dive bar has been open since the early 1980s. Stiff, inexpensive drinks and a back patio with pool tables. *Info*: 3845 5th Ave. Tel. 619/299-1911. Open daily. numberonefifth.com.

North Park
Pecs
Neighborhood bar (lots of bears) where drinks are inexpensive and you can play darts and pool. *Info*: 2046 University Ave. Tel. 619/296-0889. Closed Mon. www.pecsbar.com.

Eagle
Popular and cruisy leather bar. *Info*: 3040 North Park Way. Tel. 619/295-8072. open daily. www.sandiegoeagle.com.

Redwing Bar & Grill
A diverse crowd frequents this dive neighborhood bar. Large outdoor patio ads to the appeal. *Info*: 4012 30th St. Tel. 619/281-8700. Closed Mon and Tue. redwingbar.com.

Loma Portal
Hole in the Wall
Away from the other bars in Loma Portal, this dive bar has been around since the 1940s. Large patio, pool table, and substantial drinks. *Info*: 2820 Lytton St. Tel. 619/996-9000. Open Thu-Sun. www.theholesandiego.com.

Big Kitchen $

Breakfast and lunch at this popular South Park spot. Waffles, muffins, omelets, and plenty of vegetarian and vegan choices. The owner, Judy Forman, truly makes this a community cafe. Live music on weekends. *Info*: 3003 Grape St. Tel. 619/234-5789. Open daily. www.judysbigkitchen.com.

Lamplighter

Bring cash (no credit cards) to this dive bar located in Mission Hills. Cheap booze, retro aesthetic, friendly bartenders, and nightly karaoke makes for an interesting place to hang out. If you want to imbibe early, get there when the doors open at 6am! *Info*: 817 W. Washington St. Tel. 619/298-3624. Open daily.

Lefty's Chicago Pizzeria $-$$

This family-owned pizzeria is a little taste of Chicago in Mission Hills. Delicious Chicago-style pizza, Chicago dogs, and hearty sandwiches are on the menu. Try the deep dish pesto pie. *Info*: 4030 Goldfinch. Tel. 619/299-4030. Open daily noon-8pm. www.leftyspizza.com.

Sunnyboy Biscuit Company $-$$

Southern comfort food served in San Diego's North Park. The original Sunnyboy butterflake biscuits are served with whipped honey butter and fruit compote. The signature dish is fried chicken and biscuits (rosemary fried chicken breast on biscuits topped with maple syrup). They also have a pop-up location at the Cole Hotel in Palm Springs. *Info*: 3749 Park Blvd. Tel. 619/915-5915. Open daily 7am-2pm. www.sunnyboybiscuitco.com.

Harley Gray Kitchen & Bar $$

Breakfast, lunch, and dinner at this fun, friendly restaurant in Mission Hills. Popular brunch on weekends with free-flowing mimosas for $10. Some of the choices include lobster Benedict, chiliquiles, and prime rib. Eclectic menu where there is something every picky eater will enjoy. Nice outdoor space. *Info*: 902 West Washington St. Tel. 619/955-8451. Open daily. harleygraykitchenandbar.com.

Oscars $

Oscars, which has several locations throughout San Diego including this one in Hillcrest, is known for their fish tacos. It's not all about the tacos here as you can order fish stew, ceviche, and steak tacos, too. If you're here for breakfast, make sure you order the hearty breakfast burrito with smoked fish, bacon, ham, steak, or chorizo. Don't be put off by its strip mall location. *Info*: 646 University Ave. Tel. 619/230-5560. Open daily. Also at 703 Turquoise St. (North Pacific Beach). Tel. 858/488-6392. Open daily. And 746 Emerald St. (Pacific Beach). Tel. 858/412-4009. Open daily. www.oscarsmexicanseafood.com.

El Zarape $-$$

Order from the chalkboard menu at this small eatery in University Heights serving fresh Mexican food. When available, the lobster burrito is a must. Great shrimp tacos. *Info*: 4642 Park Blvd. Tel. 619/692-1652. Open daily. www.elzarapesandiego.com.

Civico 1845

This Italian restaurant in Little Italy features Calabrian dishes from Italy's south, including handmade pasta, pork ragu, and a vegan version of squash ravioli. Innovative dishes with vegan, vegetarian, and gluten-free options. Pinsa, an old Roman-style pizza, has toppings like burrata and mortadella. *Info*: 1845 India St. Tel. 619/431-5990. Open daily. There's also a restaurant in Banker's Hill at 2550 Fifth Ave. Tel. 619/310-5669. www.civico1845.com.

Parma Cucina Italiana $$-$$$

This cozy Italian restaurant in Hillcrest (and near Little Italy) offers fantastic Italian cuisine and an interesting collection of Italian wines. Authentic dishes like the creamy *tagliatelle alla bolognese* and the tasty lasagna are served by the Italian proprietors. Vegetarian and gluten-free dishes are available. *Info*: 3850 5th Ave. Tel. 619/543-0049. Closed Mon (lunch). www.parmaitaliankitchen.com.

Tajima Ramen $

There are several locations of this popular ramen bar. *Poke* bowls (raw fish salad), *tonkotsi* (breaded and fried pork cutlet), and, of course, ramen. Many vegetarian and vegan options. Large selection of local craft beer, wine, and house sake. Popular late night spot on weekends. *Info*: 3015 Adams Ave. (North Park). Tel 619/756-7517. Open daily. Other locations include 3739 6th Ave. in Hillcrest and 901 E St. in East Village. www.tajimasandiego.com.

Blind Lady Ale House $$

This Normal Heights ale house has 25 craft beers on tap and some are brewed in-house. You don't just come here to drink, because the Napolitano pizza is fantastic. There are plenty of other offerings like *charcuterie* boards. You'll eat at communal tables surrounded by a wall of old beer cans. Fun, friendly, and popular. *Info*: 3416 Adams Ave. Tel. 619/255-2491. Open daily. www.blindladyalehouse.com.

Mission Basilica San Diego de Alcalá

California's first mission was built in 1769 on a hill above Old Town. Soon after, natives attacked the Old Town location. As a result, the mission was moved here in 1774 and the conversion of the natives began. Native elders were concerned that their traditions would disappear. When they learned of the riches in the mission, they decided to attack. In 1775, some 800 natives burned the mission. Father Jayme, who was killed in the attack, became California's first Catholic martyr. He's buried next to the altar in the present church. In 1776, a new church was built with high protective walls and there was never another attack. The mission began to flourish with livestock, orchards, and gardens. It wasn't long before the mission was destroyed, yet again, in an 1803 earthquake. The present structure, with whitewashed adobe and stacked bell tower, was finished in 1813 and restored in 1915. *Info*: 10818 San Diego Mission Rd. in Mission Valley. Tel. 619/283-7319. Open Mon-Fri 8am-4:30pm and for Saturday evening mass and Sunday morning mass. www.missionsandiego.com. The mission is located within city limits, near the intersection of Interstate 8 and Interstate 15, and approximately one mile east of SDCCU Stadium. *See map on next page.*

Serra Mesa
llage Dr
Rancho Mission Rd
Friars Rd
Mission Gorge Rd
Zion Av
Waring Rd
College Av
SD Mission Rd
1
Alvarado Canyon Rd
8
Friars Rd
Fenton Pkwy
Rio San Diego Dr
Camino del Rio North
Camino del Rio South
mm Wy
Normal Heights
805
15
Adams Av
Aldine Dr
Fairmount Av
Montez
Monroe Av
as St
1. Mission Basilica San Diego de Alcalá

7. Further Afield

- Chula Vista
- Del Mar/Solana Beach
- Eating & Drinking in Del Mar/Solana Beach
- Encinitas/Cardiff-by-the-Sea
- Eating & Drinking in Encinitas/Cardiff-by-the-Sea
- San Diego Zoo Safari Park (Escondido)
- Eating & Drinking in Carlsbad/Oceanside

FURTHER AFIELD

There's more to the San Diego area than Dowtown and the neighborhoods. These sights are located further afield, but are all worth a visit. We'll head south to Chula Vista for some interesting sights and also north to the beaches and communities within easy reach, from Del Mar to Carlsbad.

Chula Vista

Aquatica San Diego

Owned by SeaWorld, you won't see any whale or dolphin shows here. What you will find is a wave pool, inner-tube float, water slides, and a bunch of other fun places to get totally wet! Great place to cool off in the summer heat. *Info*: 2052 Entertainment Circle (Chula Vista). Tel. 619/222-4732. Open daily Jun-Aug 10am-6pm, Apr-May and Sep-Oct Sat and Sun 10am-6pm. Admission: From $48.99. www.aquaticabyseaworld.com.

Elite Athletic Training Center

A one-mile walking tour takes you past training centers (most outside) for Olympic and Paralympic hopefuls. The training center is spread out over 155 acres. You'll pass the state-of-art facilities for track and field, archery, rugby, and more. There are more detailed guided tours available through the website. *Info*: 2800 Olympic Parkway (Chula Vista). Tel. 619/656-1500. Open Mon-Fri 9am-5pm. Tours are available on some Saturdays. Admission: $5 (Bronze Tour). www.trainatchulavista.com.

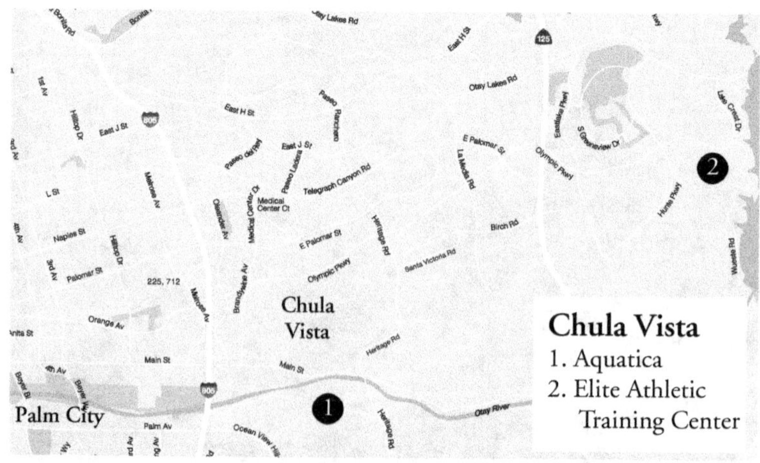

North of San Diego
Del Mar/Solana Beach
Just 30 minutes from downtown San Diego, the upscale beach town of **Del Mar** is home to the **Del Mar Racetrack**. Put on a fancy hat, and from the middle of July to the beginning of September, you can watch the races in a fabulous stadium on the coast. Gamblers (and those who just want to watch the spectacle) have been coming here since 1937. Free concerts are held after the Friday races. *Info*: 2260 Jimmy Durante Blvd. Tel 858/755-1141. Closed Mon and Tue. Admission: $6-$50. www.dmtc.com. To get to Del Mar from San Diego, take I-5 north for 20 miles (32 km) and exit at Villa de la Valle.

Also in Del Mar are the fairgrounds where the **San Diego County Fair** is held each June. *Info*: 2260 Jimmy Durante Blvd. Tel. 858/755-1161. www.delmarfairgrounds.com.

Just north of Del Mar is the quiet community of **Solana Beach**. It's known for the **Cedros Avenue Design District**, with its for high-end home decorating stores. You'll find over 85 boutiques, furniture stores, art galleries, and plenty of dining choices. *Info*: cedrosavenue.com.

Eating & Drinking in Del Mar/Solana Beach
Board & Brew $
For a quick, inexpensive bite, this shop in Del Mar (not too far from the ocean) has specialty sandwiches and craft beer. Try the baja chicken sandwich with marinated chicken breast, jalapeño peppers, and melted jack cheese. *Info*: 1212 Camino Del Mar (Del Mar). Tel. 858/481-1021. Open daily 10am-7pm. www.boardandbrew.com. Several other locations including Carlsbad and Oceanside.

Market Restaurant and Bar $$-$$$
This award-winning restaurant, bar, and lounge is located near the horse park in Del Mar. It has an interesting wine list featuring selections from California, Australia, Italy, and France. Try the crispy jidori chicken breast with a coconut-curry glaze or the striped bass with mushroom dumplings. *Info*: 3702 Via de La Valle (Del Mar). Tel. 858/523-0007. Open daily at 5:30pm. www.marketdelmar.com.

Jake's Del Mar $$-$$$
With a gorgeous coastal location, Jake's Del Mar serves eclectic American cuisine using local, sustainable products. You'll have to reserve ahead to get a table at sunset. Its Sunday brunch is extremely popular. Start with grilled prawns and dine on "Surfing Steak" (prime top sirloin, herb-grilled jumbo shrimp, and garlic whipped potatoes). Great wine list and selection of craft beers. *Info*: 1660 Coast Blvd. (Del Mar). Tel. 858/755-2002. Open daily for lunch and dinner. www.jakesdelmar.com.

Carruth Cellars $$
Laid-back urban winery and tasting room in Solana Beach. They buy grapes from vineyards in California and Oregon and do all wine production (de-stemming, crushing, fermenting, aging, and bottling) in this urban facility by the beach. *Info*: 118 S. Cedros Ave. (Solana Beach). Tel. 858/847-9463. Open daily. www.carruthcellars.com. There are also locations in Carlsbad at 2727 State St.and in the Little Italy neighborhood of San Diego at 2215 Kettner Blvd.

Encinitas/Cardiff-by-the-Sea
Only 40 minutes from downtown San Diego you'll arrive at these communities on a coastline with pristine beaches along sandstone cliffs. This is a big destination for surfers, campers, and those who just want to get away from the bustle of city life in San Diego. To reach these communities from San Diego, take I-5 north for 25 miles (40 km) and exit Birmingham Dr./Cardiff-by-the Sea or Encinitas Blvd./Encinitas.

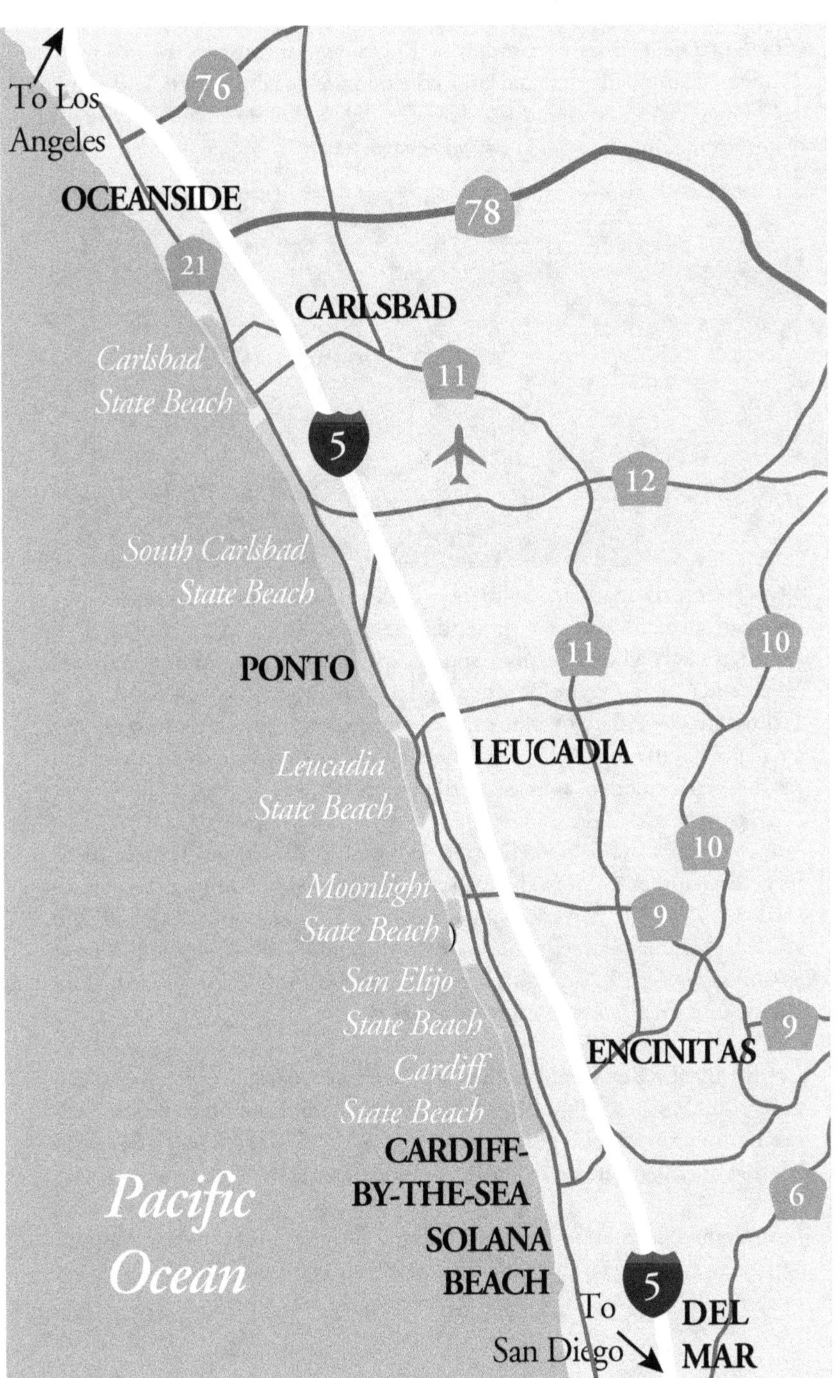
To Los Angeles
OCEANSIDE
76
21
CARLSBAD
Carlsbad State Beach
11
5
South Carlsbad State Beach
12
PONTO
11
10
LEUCADIA
Leucadia State Beach
10
Moonlight State Beach
9
San Elijo State Beach
Cardiff State Beach
ENCINITAS
9
CARDIFF-BY-THE-SEA
SOLANA BEACH
6
Pacific Ocean
5
To San Diego
DEL MAR

The **San Diego Botanic Garden** in Encinitas is a must for plant lovers. Wander around and view the large collection of bamboo, cacti, and tropical plants. *Info*: 230 Quail Gardens Dr. Tel. 858/436-3036. Open daily 9am-5pm. Admission: $14. www.sdbgarden.com.

If you want to experience Southern California beach life, head to the surf destination of **Swami's** at the end of Second Street in Encinitas. This internationally known surfing spot is named after Swami Paramahansa Yogananda, because the grounds and hermitage of the Self-Realization Fellowship (*see below*) overlook the beach. Access is primarily through the small park at the top of the cliff. There's a small parking lot, where you can head down a wooden staircase to the beach.

You can't miss the **Self-Realization Fellowship (Encinitas Temple)** with its golden domes. Next to the realization center is the calming meditation garden filled with flowers, plants, trees, and ponds with waterfalls and koi fish. The manicured gardens are on the cliff overlooking the surfers at Swami's. *Info*: 939 2nd St. (Encinitas). Tel. 760/436-7220. Closed Mon. Admission: Free. www.encinitastemple.org.

Cardiff-by-the-Sea State Beach is a popular destination for longboarders. *Info*: 2050 S. Coast Hwy. 101. The adjoining **San Elijo State Beach** has a campground overlooking the waves. *Info*: 2050 S. Coast Hwy. 101. Both beaches are open sunrise to sunset. www.parks.ca.gov.

Moonlight Beach State Park in Encinitas is another destination for sunbathers, wave-seekers, and volleyball. You'll also find a children's park here. *Info*: 400 B St. (Encinitas). Tel. 760/633-2740. www.parks.ca.gov.

Eating & Drinking in Encinitas and Cardiff-by-the-Sea
Swami's $
This eatery is named for the famous surf spot across Highway 101. There are nine locations throughout the San Diego area, but this is the original. Highly popular brunch. Grab a table on the outdoor patio and smell the ocean air while enjoying breakfast burritos, acai bowls, and veggie hash. *Info*: 1163 S Coast Hwy. 101 (Encinitas). Tel. 760/944-0612. Open daily 7am-4pm. wwwswamiscafe.com.

Haggo's Organic Taco $
This "shack" is known for its fish tacos. Organic ingredients are used in all of the dishes, including vegan nachos, grass-fed beef tacos, and chicken rice lime soup. *Info*: 1302 N Coast Hwy. 101 (Encinitas/Leucadia). Tel. 760/753-6000. Open Tue-Sun 11am-5pm. Closed Mon. www.haggosorganictaco.com.

Pacific Coast Grill $$$
This is *the* place to experience fine dining and the beautiful sunset. Try to grab a table on the patio overlooking Cardiff State Beach. Start with the lobster and shrimp chowder with smoked bacon, and for your main course, how about grilled wild salmon or chile-rubbed filet mignon and lobster? *Info*: 2526 S. Coast Hwy. 101 (Cardiff-by-the-Sea). Tel. 760/479-0721. Open daily for lunch and dinner. www.pacificcoastgrill.com.

Carlsbad/Oceanside
Carlsbad is quintessential Southern California, with seven miles of sunny coastline, nine craft breweries, world-class resorts, shopping, golf, restaurants, and Legoland, its most popular destination. **Oceanside** has several note-

worthy sights and is five miles (8 km) north and next to Camp Pendleton Marine Corps Base. *Info*: Carlsbad is 35 miles (56 km) north of downtown San Diego on I-5 North. Exit at Carlsbad Village Drive. www.visitcarlsbad.com. Oceanside is 40 miles (64 km) north of San Diego. To visit downtown Oceanside, exit Mission Ave.

Legoland

Not just interlocking building blocks here, but 60 rides, shows, 4D movie theater, a summer water park, and the Sea Life Aquarium. Hugely popular for kids! *Info*: 1 Legoland Dr. (Carlsbad). Tel. 760/918-5346. Open daily from 10am. Admission: From $95 (check the website for frequent deals). www.legoland.com.

The Flower Fields

For six to eight weeks a year (from early March to early May), Mother Nature transforms these 50 acres into an incredible display of color. The flower featured here is the Giant Tecolote Ranunculus, with large, double-petaled blooms on tall, straight stems. *Info*: 5704 Paseo Del Norte (Carlsbad). Tel. 760/431-0352. Open 9am-6pm Mar-early May. Admission: $20, $18 age 60 plus, $10 ages 3-10. wwwtheflowerfields.com. From downtown San Diego, I-5 North to Palomar Airport Road exit. Head east (right turn) on Palomar Airport Road. Go one block to Paseo Del Norte and turn left.

Museum of Making Music

Hundreds of vintage and modern instruments are housed in this museum. You'll hear pieces from the marches of the early 1900s through the times of jazz, folk, rock 'n roll, and pop. *Info*: 5790 Armada Dr. (Carlsbad). Tel. 760/438-5996. Open Tue-Sun 10am-5pm. Closed Mon. www.museumofmakingmusic.org. *The museum is currently closed for renovations and should reopen in 2021.*

The Miniature Engineering Craftsmanship Museum

This special interest museum features wood and metalworking craftsmanship. Here you'll find airplanes, ships, vehicles, clocks, jewelry, guns, and dollhouses. There's a workshop where you can see how these small objects are created. You'll be amazed at the precision it takes to create these models. *Info*: 3190 Lionshead Ave. (Carlsbad). Tel. 760/727-9492. Open Thu-Sat 9:30am-4pm. www.craftmanshipmuseum.com.

Leo Carrillo Ranch

Carrillo was a character actor, and conservationist, best known for playing Pancho in the popular television series *The Cisco Kid* in the 1950s. He purchased this 19th-century hacienda in 1937. Secluded in a 27-acre canyon, this park contains adobe buildings, antique windmills, a reflecting pool, and other historic structures. You can stroll through the meticulously landscaped garden, which is home to native plants, peacocks, and bird of paradise. *Info*: 6200 Flying Leo Carillo Lane (Carlsbad). Tel. 760/476-1042. Open daily 9am-5pm. Admission: Free. Guided tours available. carillo-ranch.org.

California Surf Museum

This small museum tells the history of surfing, including everything from wood to plastic surfboards. Exhibits feature international surfing stars and the cautionary story of Bethany Hamilton, who lost her arm in a tiger shark attack. *Info*: 312 Pier View Way (Oceanside). Tel. 760/721-6876. Open daily 10am-4pm. Admission: $7; $5 age 62 plus, military, students; 12 and under free. wwwsurfmuseum.org.

Mission San Luis Rey de Francia

This site was founded by a French missionary in 1798. The restored church features whitewashed walls, a long corridor with 32 Roman arches, carved wooden doors, colorful painted walls and murals, and the original baptismal font of hammered copper. It was named for King Louis IX of France and has the nickname "King of the Missions" as it is the largest of the 21 Franciscan missions in California. You can take a tour to learn about the history of the mission ($12). *Info*: 4050 Mission Ave. (Oceanside). Tel. 760/757-3651.

Open Mon-Fri 9:30am-5pm, Sat and Sun 10am-5pm. Admission: $7, 65 plus $5, $3, 6-18, free under 6 and active military. www.sanluisrey.org.

Marine Corps Mechanized Museum
If you've ever wanted to get access to the Marine Corps Base Camp Pendleton, you can by visiting this museum. A unique collection of more than 60 vehicles (tanks, armored trucks, all terrain, and ambulances) from World War I to present. They're housed in a terminal building used since World War II as a training arrival point for Marines. *Info*: 6212 Vandegrift Blvd. (Camp Pendleton/Oceanside). Tel. 760/725-5758. Open Mon-Thu 8am-4pm, Fri 8am-1pm. Closed Sat and Sun. Note that you will need an ID for everyone in your vehicle and current vehicle registration and proof of insurance. www.themech.org.

Oceanside Museum of Art
This museum houses art focused on works by contemporary artists of Southern California. Everything including paintings, sculptures, furniture, quilts, and glass. Exhibits change several times a year. *Info*: 704 Pier Way (Oceanside). Tel 760/435-3720. Closed Mon. Admission: $8. www.oma-online.org.

SAN DIEGO ZOO SAFARI PARK
(Escondido)
This large wildlife sanctuary, associated with the San Diego Zoo, is home to more than 3,000 animals and more than 300 species. Over half of the 1,800 acres have been set aside as protected native species habitat. You can upgrade your visit by purchasing a safari tour for an up-close look at the animals. One-hour safari tours start at $419 (per truck, for a group of up to six household members). *Info*: 15500 San Pasqual Valley Rd. (Escondido). Tel. 760/747-8702. Open daily 9am-5pm (hours vary by season). Admission: $60 (day pass), $50 ages 3-11. www.sdzsafaripark.org. To get to Escondido from downtown San Diego, take I-15 North for 30 miles (48 km) to the Via Rancho Parkway exit 27. Go east and follow signs to the park.

Eating & Drinking in Carlsbad/Oceanside

Campfire $$-$$$

This restaurant in Carlsbad Village has a large outdoor patio, fire pits, and a wood-fired kitchen. Dishes include seabass, cavatelli with duck, and delicious grilled half chicken. In keeping with the campfire theme, they also have s'mores. Interesting wine menu that is heavy on Californian selections and a rotating list of craft beers. *Info*: 2725 State St. (Carlsbad). Tel. 760/637-5121. Open daily. www.thisiscampfire.com.

Paon $$$

Innovative French cuisine with Californian influences at this popular restaurant and wine bar in Carlsbad Village. Elegant Art Deco decor, but try to score a seat on the lovely outdoor patio. Locally grown produce and organic meat, game, and fish are featured on its changing menu. Start with the escargot bourguignon served with herb garlic butter, and for your main course try the pan-roasted Pacific king salmon or roasted New Zealand venison. We like the wine bar/bistro menu. Interesting wine list that features Californian and international selections. *Info*: 2975 Roosevelt St. (Carlsbad). Tel. 760/729-7377. Open daily. www.paoncarlsbad.com.

Beach Plum Kitchen $-$$

Locals and tourists mingle for breakfast, lunch, and brunch at this locally owned eatery in Carlsbad. It's casual and comfortable, with both indoor and outdoor dining. You'll have a full stomach after you down the fried chicken and waffles, hearty breakfast burrito, or coconut-almond crusted French toast for breakfast. Lunch features a New England lobster roll and Ahi tuna salad. Lots of vegetarian and gluten-free options. *Info*: 6971 El Camino Real (Carlsbad). Tel. 760/931-1362. Open daily for breakfast and lunch. beachplumkitchen.com.

Beach Break Cafe $-$$

The decor here is surf-inspired, which is appropriate for its location on Highway 101 in Oceanside along the fabulous California coast. It's especially popular for breakfast, where you'll dive into the cinnamon-laced coffee cake, banana crunch French toast, or substantial omelets. Lunch offers sandwiches, including the mahi-mahi burrito. *Info*: 1802 South Coast Hwy. 101 (Oceanside). Tel. 760/439-6355. Open daily 7am-2pm. beachbreakcafe.com.

Local Tap House & Kitchen $$

Don't just come here for the local craft brews, because the food is worth the visit. There's a good collection of Californian wines by the glass. Popular brunch, especially in good weather on the large patio. You can dine on everything from a blackened tuna club sandwich to short rib French dip. It's known for its delicious deviled eggs. Fun and friendly choice in Oceanside. *Info*: 308 S. South Coast Hwy. (Oceanside). Tel. 760/547-1469. Open daily. www.localtaphouse.com.

Wrench and Rodent Seabasstropub

Okay, the name is weird and the decor a bit odd, but you're coming to this eatery in Oceanside for some innovative and creative sushi. Everything is locally sourced. It's a laid-back affair (wear your flip-flops) and you can relax with a local craft beer, sake, or a glass of wine from one of California's lesser-known vineyards. Try the shrimp tempura roll in a spicy berry sauce. Lots of vegan options, too. *Info*: 1815 South Coast Hwy. (Oceanside). Tel. 760/271-0531. Open daily. www.seabasstropub.com.

8. Excursions

- Temecula
- Julian
- Borrego Springs/
Anza-Borrego Desert State Park
- Tijuana, Mexico

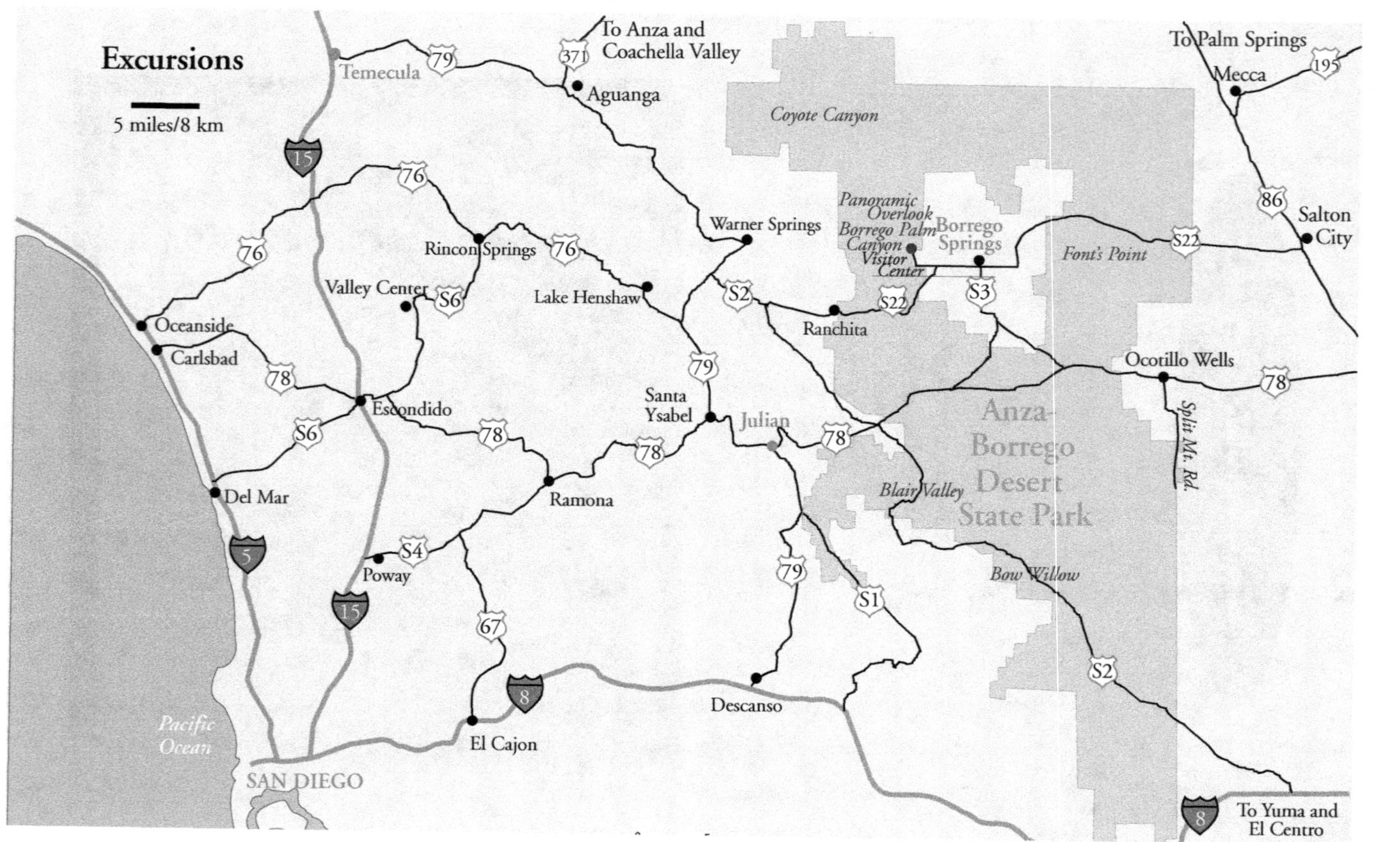
Excursions
5 miles/8 km
Temecula
79
To Anza and Coachella Valley
371
Aguanga
To Palm Springs
Mecca
195
Coyote Canyon
15
76
Panoramic Overlook
Borrego Palm Canyon Visitor Center
Borrego Springs
86
Salton City
76
Rincon Springs
76
Warner Springs
S22
S3
Font's Point
S22
Valley Center
S6
Lake Henshaw
S2
Ranchita
Oceanside
Ocotillo Wells
Carlsbad
78
79
Anza-Borrego Desert State Park
Split Mt. Rd.
78
Escondido
78
Santa Ysabel
Julian
78
S6
78
Del Mar
Ramona
Blair Valley
Bow Willow
5
S4
79
Poway
S1
15
Bow Willow
67
S2
8
Descanso
Pacific Ocean
SAN DIEGO
El Cajon
8
To Yuma and El Centro

TEMECULA

From San Diego take I-15 North to exit 58 CA-79 North/Temecula Pkwy. in Temecula. One-hour drive. You can also reach Temecula by Greyhound Bus from the station downtown in East Village at 1313 National Ave. between 13th St. and 14th St. The trip takes about an hour. One-way is $20.

Just one hour away from downtown San Diego is the Temecula Valley wine region. You can tour nearly 50 wineries, stroll through historic Old Town, head to a casino, take a hot air balloon ride, or play a round of golf. The valley is surrounded by mountains and is known for its beautiful weather. Most wineries have panoramic views of the rolling hills filled with vineyards.

Old Town Temecula

Touristy Old Town dates back to 1859 and has an Old West feel. You can stroll the sidewalks (made of wooden railroad ties) through blocks of boutiques, gift shops, souvenir shops, restaurants, and antique stores. Befitting its reputation as a wine destination, there are plenty of tasting rooms, and wine bars and shops (and craft breweries for you beer lovers).

The popular year-round **Certified Farmer's Market** is held on Saturdays. On weekends, there is live entertainment at many of the venues, especially at **Old Town Temecula Community Theater** (temeculaca.gov/theater). *Info*: Old Town Front St. between Morena Rd. and 1st St. www.visittemeculavalley.com.

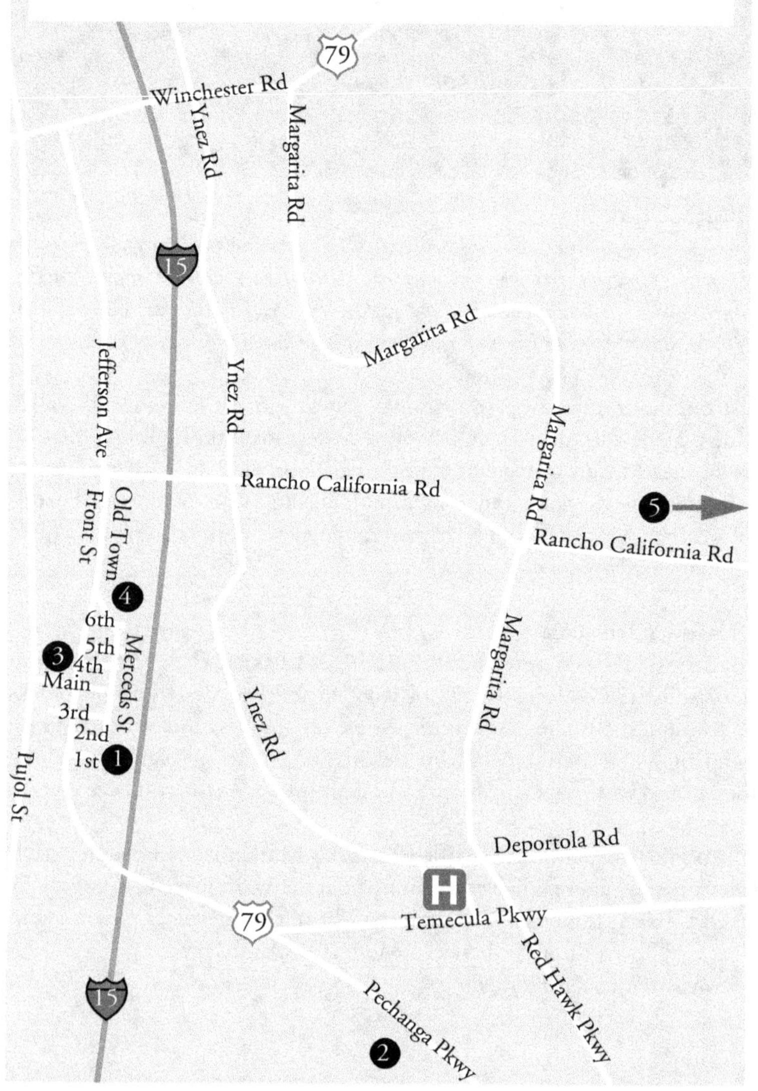

Temecula
1. Old Town
2. Pechange Resort
3. Temecula Children's Museum
4. Temecula Valley Museum
5. Wineries
Winchester Rd
79
Ynez Rd
Margarita Rd
15
Margarita Rd
Jefferson Ave
Ynez Rd
Rancho California Rd
Margarita Rd
5
Rancho California Rd
Front St
Old Town
4
6th
Mercedes St
Margarita Rd
5th
3
4th
Main
3rd
Ynez Rd
2nd
1st
1
Pujol St
Deportola Rd
H
79
Temecula Pkwy
Red Hawk Pkwy
15
Pechanga Pkwy
2

Pechanga Resort and Casino

This is California's largest casino, featuring a large bingo parlor, thousands of slot machines, and hundreds of table games. It's also a destination for live entertainment at its theater and comedy club. The hotel has over 1,000 rooms and the complex includes several bars, a spa, pools, and 10 restaurants. *Info*: 45000 Pechanga Pkwy. Tel. 951/693-1819. www.pechanga.com.

Temecula Valley Museum

Explore the history of the region through artifacts, cultural items, ranching and farming equipment, documents, and photographs. One exhibit features the native inhabitants, the Luiseño Indians. There's also a discovery area for children featuring hands-on exhibits in a Western street setting with a general store, a dress shop, a photographer's studio, and a ride-a-pony station. *Info*: 28314 Mercedes St. (Old Town). Tel. 951/694-6450. Open Tue-Sun 10am-4pm. Closed Mon. Admission: Suggested donation $5 per person/$10 per family. Free parking. www.temeculavalleymuseum.org.

Temecula Children's Museum/Pennypickle's Workshop

Popular with school field trips, this quirky museum offers an interactive tour through the home of fictitious inventor Professor Phineas T. Pennypickle. Exhibits let kids discover science by experiencing an earthquake, learning chemistry in the kitchen, playing a musical instrument, and walking through a glow-in-the-dark maze. Visits are for two-hour sessions. *Info*: 42081 Main St. Tel. 951/308-6376. Closed Mon. Admission: $10 (children), $5 adults. www.pennypickles.org.

Hot Air Balloon Rides

Hot air ballooning is a popular attraction in Temecula. Weather permitting, rides are available year-round at sunrise only, due to afternoon and evening winds. You can take in a panoramic view of the surrounding mountains, vineyards, and expansive estates. The **Temecula Valley Balloon and Wine Festival**, held every June, is the largest hot air balloon festival in the state. The skies are filled with colorful balloons. The festival features wine tastings, food, and concerts. There are many companies that offer balloon rides. Here are a few:

• **California Dreamin' Balloon Adventures** operates from the Vindemia Winery, 33133 Vista Del Monte Rd., Tel. 951/699-0601. From $168. Ages 7 and up. www.californiadreamin.com.

• **Magical Adventure Balloon Rides** departs from the South Coast Winery Resort and Spa. Tel. 951/699-5800. From $129. Flight lasts one hour, but the experience is three hours. There's a post-flight celebration with champagne, juice, or mimosa toast, continental breakfast with an assortment of breakfast items. www.hotairfun.com/temecula.

• **Temecula Balloon Rides** departs from Perris Airport in the Temecula Valley. Tel. 951/678-6386. Admission: From $117. Includes pastries, hot and cold drinks, and post-flight champagne. www.temeculaballoonrides.net.

Wineries

In the 19th century, the majority of wine in California came from Southern California. Eventually the Northern California wine country overtook the Temecula Valley. In the 1960s, Temecula led the way in the revival of vine culture in Southern California. These wines along with Temecula's fantastic climate and beautiful setting have made the area a popular destination for visitors. Temecula has nearly 50 licensed wineries and 70 growers that farm vineyards throughout Temecula Valley. We've highlighted a few of our favorites. For a full list of wineries in Temecula, visit www.visittemeculavalley.com.

Avensole

Avensole is a word comprised of "avventura" (Italian for adventure) and "sole" (for "one of a kind" or "matchless"). This lesser-known winery is located in a sprawling hilltop estate with views across Temecula Wine Country. The open-air restaurant is relaxed and comfortable. *Info*: 34567 Rancho California Rd. Tel. 951/252-2003. Tasting Room open daily 11am-5pm. Restaurant closed Tue, Wed, and Mon (dinner). www.avensolewinery.com.

Callaway Vineyard and Winery

One of the oldest in the valley, this vineyard produces a dozen varietals from Cabernet Sauvignon to Chardonnay. You can tour the winery and then enjoy a wine flight on the terrace while you take in views of Temecula's wine country. The on-site restaurant **Meritage** (Closed Mon and Tue. Tel 951/587-8889) offers farm-to-table meals paired with Callaway's award-winning wines, *Info*: 32720 Rancho California Rd. Tel. 951/676-4001. Open daily 10:30am-6pm. www.callawaywinery.org.

Lorenzi Estate

This wine estate is on the smaller side of the wineries in the area. Peaceful, quiet, and friendly, you won't find many of the bridal parties and bus tours here as you might in other spots. This limited production winery is heavy on reds, but also has whites to choose from. You can enjoy your wine in the beautiful flower garden. *Info*: 36095 Monte De Oro Rd. Tel. 951/506-1300. Tasting room open daily 11am-5pm. www.lorenziestatewines.com.

Mount Palomar Winery

One of the oldest wineries in the valley dates back to 1969 and led the way to the revival of vine culture in the region. Located on 315 acres, Palomar produces a range of fine wines with an emphasis on Bordeaux and Italian varieties. They also produce port and cream sherry. The restaurant here (Closed Mon and Tue) pairs the wines with American fusion dining. *Info*: 33829 Rancho California Rd. Tel. 951/676-5047. Open daily 11am-5pm (Fri and Sat until 7pm). www.mountpalomar.com.

South Coast Winery

This winery has a spa, resort, and restaurant. Hugely popular, you won't be disappointed with its award-winning vintages that include merlot, syrah, and cabernet. The sister winery, **Carter Estate Winery** (www.carterestatewinery.com) is across the street and known for its sparkling wines produced in the *méthode champenoise* (the traditional method used to produce champagne). *Info*: 34843 Rancho California Rd. Tel. 877/743-8303. Open daily 10am-6pm. www.southcoastwinery.com.

Horses

Not only is the Temecula Valley wine country, but it's also horse country. **Galway Downs** features horse races and dressage events at a complex with over 240 acres. *Info*: 38801 Los Corralitos Rd. (off CA Hwy. 79). Tel. 951/303-0405. www.galwaydowns.com. You can combine drinking wine and riding in a carriage with the wine tours offered by **Temecula Carriage Company**. *Info*: 40001 Berenda Rd. Tel. 844/369-1852. Open daily 8am-8pm. From $165 per couple. www.temeculacarriageco.com.

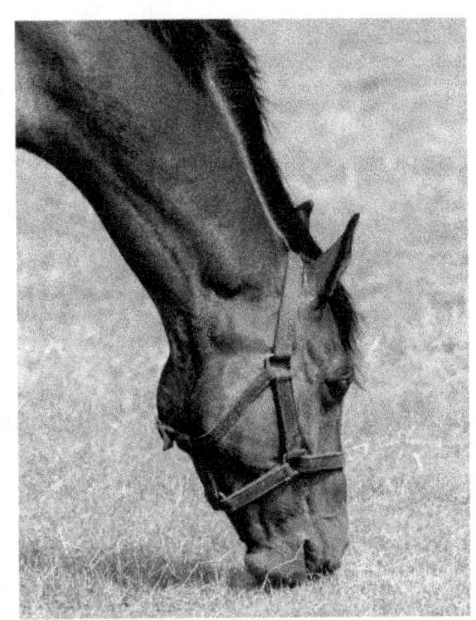

And, if you'd like to ride a horse, you can journey on trails connecting vineyards with **Wine Country Trails by Horseback**. *Info*: 34225 Rancho California Rd. (Maurice Carrie Winery). Tel. 951/506-8706. Open Wed-Sun. From $100. Visit www.winecountrytrailsbyhorseback.com for reservations.

Eating & Drinking in Temecula

Most wineries have fantastic restaurants with wonderful views of the rolling hills (*see the Winery section*). Here are a few other suggestions.

Trattoria Toscana $$-$$$

Don't be put off by the location of this popular Italian restaurant in a strip mall. Authentic Italian cuisine is served in this friendly trattoria. Try the gnocchi in a creamy gorgonzola sauce or the grilled filet mignon topped with a porcini mushroom cream sauce. The house wine is from Temecula, but there are plenty of choices from most wine regions of Italy. *Info*: 26485 Ynez Rd., Suites M and N. Tel. 951/296-2066. Closed Tue and Wed. www.trattoriatoscanaintemecula.com.

Gambling Cowboy $$-$$$

This Western-style chophouse is located in Old Town. Casual dining includes classic steak and seafood choices. The wine list features local and international choices. The saloon menu offers less expensive options like a 10-ounce steak burger. Try to get a seat on the third floor deck with sweeping views of the valley. *Info*: 42072 5th St. Tel. 951/699-2895. Closed Mon. www.ilovethecowboy.com.

The Goat & Vine $$

Rustic-chic kitchen in Old Town serving thin-crust pizza, sandwiches ,and wraps. The innovative pizzas include the jalapeño lime carnitas pizza topped with roasted pork shoulder, mozzarella, green onions, jalapeños, and avocados. The wine selection features local wineries and a delicious watermelon sangria. *Info*: 41923 2nd St. #103. Tel. 951/695-5600. www.thegoatandvine.com.

Swing Inn Cafe $-$$

This diner, complete with red vinyl booths, is located in the heart of Old Town. Hearty breakfast dishes, like pork chops and eggs, are served all day. They have a giant cinnamon roll and a strong Bloody Mary. You might opt for the country fried steak for dinner. *Info*: 28676 Old Town Front Rd. Tel. 951/676-2321. Open daily. www.swinginncafe.com.

JULIAN

Located 60 miles northeast of San Diego. From San Diego take I-8 East for 25 miles. Then take California Highway 79 North for 25 miles.

In 1869 Frederick Coleman, a former slave from Kentucky, discovered gold in a creek. He founded a gold mine and others began arriving in search of the precious metal. This mountain town is named after the Julian brothers, former Confederate soldiers, who arrived from Georgia and also established a mine. Gold fever lasted about 30 years. Unlike others that turned to ghost towns, Julian thrived as an agricultural center. Apple trees planted here became the new "gold" of the region. Today, Julian apples are sought after for pies and cider.

The village is a destination for day trips and weekend getaways for many from San Diego and Los Angeles. So, be warned that during weekends and festival time it's crowded and parking can be tricky. Crowds are also present during the height of apple-picking season and when fall colors explode. www.visitjulian.com.

Eagle Mining Company

The Eagle Mining Company offers tours of Julian's original gold mines. Guides lead you through 1,000 feet of tunnels into the gold mine. You can pan for gold and learn about the milling and extraction process. *Info*: 2320 C St. Tel. 760/765-0036. Open Mon-Fri 10am-4pm, Sat and Sun 10am-5pm. Admission: $10, $5 ages 5-13. www.theeaglemining.com.

Pioneer Museum

Vintage clothing, photographs, household items, and mining equipment are used to explore the history of Julian. The building was constructed in 1890 as a blacksmith shop, and later served as a brewery. There's an exhibit of the Native American inhabitants as well as Victorian era pianos, the original city buggy and sleigh, and mounted animals found in the area. *Info*: 2811 Washington St. Tel. 760/765-0227. Open Thu-Sun 10am-4pm. Admission: $5. www.julianpioneermuseum.org.

Julian Pioneer Cemetery

This cemetery dates back to the 1870s, but it's the location that makes it worth a visit. The cemetery provides its permanent "residents" with a panoramic view of the countryside. *Info*: Farmer Rd. at A St. (at the north end of Main St.). Open daily sunrise to sunset. www.juliancemetery.org.

California Wolf Center

Home to several packs of gray wolves. Its mission is to prevent the extinction of some of the rarest land mammals in the world. Tours of the resident wolf packs are by appointment only. If you don't take a tour, the downtown visitor center and nature store is open to all. It has exhibits on wolf biology and ecology. *Info*: 2775 B St. Tel. 760/765-0030. Open daily 10am-5pm. Tours from $30. Reservations at www.californiawolfcenter.org.

> **PICKING**
> Apple and pear picking is a popular activity in the late summer and early fall in and around Julian. These orchards are open on weekends and take cash only.
> • **Apple Starr**: 1020 Julian Orchard Dr. Tel. 760/305-2169. $25 picking bag (one peck/12 lbs), $15 additional bag per family member.
> www.apple-starr.com.
> • **Calico Ranch**: 4200 Highway 78. Tel. 858/586-0392. Family-run apple and pear orchard. $10 for a 1/4 peck/7 lbs.
> www.calicoranch.com.

Eating & Drinking in Julian

Julian Pie Company $

Apples, apples, and more apples. That's what Julian is all about. This shop is popular with both locals and visitors. The original apple pie is the favorite, but there are also others here like the delicious apple mountain berry crumb. You can't visit the city without trying one of its word-famous pies. *Info*: 2225 Main St. Tel. 760/765-2449. Open daily 9am-5pm. www.julianpie.com.

Soups and Such Cafe $-$$

This comfortable cafe is right on Main Street. The menu features home-made soups (try the hearty vegetable soup), sandwiches and salads at lunch. Breakfast (Thursday to Sunday) includes eggs Benedict and organic apple pancakes. Local wine and cider is also served. *Info*: 2000 Main St. Tel. 760/765-4761. Closed Tue. Facebook: Soups and Such Cafe.

Julian Station

Julian Station features three tasting room experiences: Julian Hard Cider, Julian Wine & Chocolate, and The Cooler Craft Beer Tap & Tasting Room. The Station is also home to Colt's Burger Bar, serving grass-fed beef, bison, and portobello burgers. There are also several shops and boutiques showcasing local art, gifts, and antiques. Frequent live music performances. *Info*: 4470 Julian Rd. (Hwy. 78). Tel. 760/885-8364. Open daily. www.julianstation.com.

BORREGO SPRINGS/ANZA-BORREGO DESERT STATE PARK

San Diego to Borrego Springs is an 80-mile drive. Take I-8 East for 25 miles, then north on Highway 79 for 25 miles. At Julian, take California Highway 78 East for 30 miles. Make sure your car has a full tank of gas and that you have food and water, as there are no facilities in the park. And never forget you're in the desert—so cell-phone service isn't always reliable!

California's largest state park is spread over 600,000 acres of desert. The area is named for Spanish explorer Juan Bautista de Anza and for *borrego*, Spanish for sheep, as the area is home to the majestic bighorn sheep. Visitors come to get away from the city and experience palm oases, desert cacti, hiking trails, and fossel hunting. Roughly five million years ago, a tropical sea flooded the region. The abundance of life forms from that sea are preserved as fossils. Its biggest draw is the wonderful desert bloom in spring, where visitors grab their phones to take photos of desert flora like colorful poppies, purple sand verbena, and yellow sunflowers. March is usually the best time to experience the desert boom, but you can get an updated report by calling the Wildflower Hotline at 760-767-4684. After the bloom, summers here can be brutal with temperatures well over 100 degrees F (38 C).

On your way into the park outside Borrego Springs is **Galleta Meadows**. Artist Ricardo Breceda has filled the area with 130 large metal sculptures of prehistoric animals like dinosaurs, desert animals like bighorn sheep, and a 350-foot-long dragon. *Info*: 1700-1844 Borrego Springs Rd. Tel/760/767-5555.

The town of **Borrego Springs** is completely surrounded by the state park. The park's **Visitor Center** here is built partially underground to help keep it cool in the desert summers. The helpful center will guide you through visiting the top sights in the area and the many hiking opportunities. A desert garden surrounds the Visitor Center. *Info*: 300 Palm Canyon Dr. Tel. 760/767-5311. Visitor Center is open daily Oct-May 9am-5pm, Jun-Sep weekends and holidays. Park is open daily dawn to dusk. www.theabf.org and www.parks.ca.gov. Some of the highlights of the park are:

• **Borrego Palm Canyon**: From Palm Canyon Campground, you can hike to Borrego Palm Canyon on the Palm Canyon Nature Trail. This three-mile (5 km) popular route takes you to a creek that feeds an oasis of California fan palms, the only palm native to the state.

• **Panoramic Overlook**: Between the Visitor Center and the Borrego Palm Canyon is this fantastic place to take in the desert landscape and the colorful sunset. It's a 1.5 mile (2.4 km) uphill hike from the Palm Canyon Campground.

• **Font's Point**: This overlook into the badlands provides spectacular views of the desert for miles. To get here, take Palm Canyon Road (S-22) east from the Visitor Center. At 10 miles, turn right (south) onto the dirt road where there is a sign for Font's Point. You'll drive for about four miles on a dirt road (four-wheel-drive vehicle is necessary much of the time because of soft sand) until you reach a lot where you can park and take a short walk to the viewpoint.

• **Coyote Canyon**: This area is comprised of 75,600 acres of the northern section of the park. This was the site of an ancient Cahuilla Indian village. It's closed from June to September to allow wildlife (especially bighorn sheep) to have access to the seasonal creeks that flow through the region. Coyote Canyon can be accessed from Borrego Springs at the end of Horse Camp Road and DiGiorgio Road. When not closed, visitors have access to 35 miles of the canyon for hiking, biking, horseback riding, and off-road adventures. Four-wheel drive vehicles are needed to access most of the canyon.

• **Bow Wow**: This was once the travel route used by the Cahuilla Indians to escape the heat of the desert and reach their summer home in the nearby Laguna Mountains. The hikes to Mountain Palm Springs, Carrizo Badlands Overlook, and Rockhouse Canyon Loop begin at the Bow Willow Campground located off California Highway S2 about 20 miles north of I-8. You'll find spring-fed oases and an abundance of desert plants (especially California fan palms). This is an excellent hiking area.

• **Blair Valley**: The Native American tribes that once lived here left pictographs and petroglyphs on boulders and cliffs. To see these 2,000-year-old Native American artworks, head to the Pictograph Trail in Little Blair Valley. Drive on the dirt road to the trailhead. From there you can walk to the pictographs. Blair Valley is on S2, seven miles south of California Highway 78.

• **Split Mountain:** At the southeast corner of the park off California Highway 78 is this aptly named destination that looks just like a mountain split in half. Erosion and earthquakes created this natural phenomenon. You can drive, especially if your vehicle has four-wheel drive, for four miles (6.5 km) through the canyon.

If you're spending the night here, and not camping, **Borrego Springs Resort $$-$$$** has a restaurant, golf course, spa, pools, and tennis courts. *Info*: 1112 Tilting T Dr. Tel. 760/767-5700. www.borregospringsresort.com. There are only 15 rooms at **Borrego Valley Inn $$$** with private patios, fireplaces, desert gardens, swimming pools, and excellent views of the desert landscape. *Info*: 405 Palm Canyon Dr. Tel. 760/767-0311. www.highwaywestvacations.com. The budget choice here is downtown at **Stanlunds Resort Inn $-$$** with standard motel rooms and a pool. *Info*: 2771 Borrego Springs Rd. Tel. 760/767-5501. www.stanlunds.com. **The Palms at Indian Head $$** offers Mid-Century Modern architecture and a lovely pool. Cary Grant and Marilyn Monroe have stayed here. *Info*: 2320 Hoberg Rd. Tel. 760/767-7788. www.thepalmsatindianhead.com. The hotel restaurant **Coyote Steakhouse $$-$$$** serves steaks, chops, and seafood. The hotel has an arrangement (and discount coupon) with the nearby casual restaurant **Red Ocotillo $$** that serves pasta, sandwiches, burgers, and salads. *Info*: 721 Avenida Sureste. Tel. 760/767-7400. Open daily for breakfast, lunch, and dinner. www.redocotillo.com. Another eating option is standard bar fare at **Big Horn Burgers and Shakes $$** with Western decor. It's located at the **Palm Canyon Hotel & RV Resort $-$$** where you can rent a room, park your RV, or stay in an Airstream trailer. *Info*: 221 Palm Canyon Dr. Tel. 760/767-5341. www.highwaywestvacations.com.

PALM SPRINGS MADE EASY

From Borrego Springs, you're 86 miles (138 km) from **Palm Springs** and the **Coachella Valley**, 29 miles (47 km) to **Salton City** and the **Salton Sea**, and 118 miles (189 km) to **Joshua Tree National Park and the towns of the Hi-Desert**. These exciting destinations are all explored in our *Palm Springs Made Easy* book (*see p. 120*).

TIJUANA, MEXICO

Tijuana, with a population of nearly two million, is only 20 miles south of San Diego. Park your car on the U.S. side of the border and then cross on foot. You'll need your passport, and be prepared for any bag you're carrying to be inspected. Taxis are available once you cross the border.

One of the first things you'll see when you enter is the massive Mexican flag. Once through the border, most head directly to **Avenida Revolución**, the main thoroughfare of the historic downtown (**Zona Centro**). This is the main tourist area with shopping, markets, casinos, bars, and clubs. You'll find plenty of souvenir shops and "zonkeys," donkeys painted with stripes to make them look like zebras. You need to pay to have your picture taken with them! Colorful Mexican crafts like jewelry, pottery, blankets, and ceramics are available along the avenue. Most places take both pesos and U.S. dollars, and note that many smaller shops and restaurants do not take credit cards. Get ready to haggle! Towering above all of it is the **Tijuana Arch** (**El Arco del Milenio**) constructed in 2000. Below the arch is Plaza Santa Cecilia, the original center of the city. Street art in Tijuana includes interesting sculpture and colorful graffiti and murals.

If you want to experience some Mexican culture, head to **CECUT/Centro Cultural Tijuana**, a cultural center with rotating art exhibits and dance and musical performances. They also have a huge IMAX theater. *Info*: 9350 Paseo de los Héroes. Open daily 9am-9pm. Admission: $3. www.cecut.gob.mx.

Many come here just for the food. Tijuana is known for its street food, but there are plenty of restaurants too. The tacos served at *taquerias* are inexpensive and fresh. *Cantinas* and bars serve excellent drinks made with tequila, especially margaritas. You may want to purchase a bottle to take back to San Diego. By the way, the legal drinking age is 18.

The city is known for its nightlife. **La Sexta** has a collection of clubs and bars. By the way, "sexta" doesn't mean sex, but is named for Calle Sexta (Sixth Street) as this area is along Calle Sexta at Avenida Revolución. If you're looking for sex, the red-light district is in Zona Norte (north of Calle Primera) but quite dangerous. We would be remiss if we didn't mention crime and safety. Tijuana has a reputation of being seedy, but simple precautions like not flashing money, dressing modestly, and not leaving the tourist area will go a long way.

9. Sleeping

SLEEPING

Many visitors to San Diego rent a home or condo through short-term rental sites. The city has very strict guidelines on short-term rentals, including heavy fines for violating the rules (like noise). This chapter highlights some of the city's best places to sleep by neighborhood.

SLEEPING PRICES

Prices for two people in a double room:
- Expensive: over $200
- Moderate: $100-200
- Inexpensive: under $100

Hotels

Balboa Park

Inn at the Park $$

This 82-unit hotel was built in 1926 as an apartment building, so offers studio, one bedroom, and two bedroom suites. It has a great location across the street from Balboa Park and within easy walking distance of the nightlife and restaurants in the Hillcrest neighborhood. Kitchens are stocked with glassware, plates, utensils, cookware, coffee makers, microwaves, apartment-sized refrigerators, and stovetops. There's a laundry room, fitness center, and a rooftop sun deck. Great for long-term stays. *Info*: 525 Spruce St. Tel. 619/291-0999. www.shellhospitality.com/Inn-at-the-park.

Downtown

Horton Grand $$$

A boutique hotel comprised of two adjoining 1880s buildings connected by a courtyard. Victorian charm with antique furniture and marble-framed fireplaces in each room. You'll have modern amenities like WiFi, coffee makers, and flat-screen televisions. *Info*: 311 Island Ave. Tel. 619/544-1886. www.hortongrand.com.

Omni San Diego $$$

This luxury high-rise hotel has rooms that overlook Petco Park and there's even a sky bridge to the stadium. You're also just across the street from the Convention Center. Enjoy the rooftop pool and bar with views of Coronado. You're near all the nightlife and restaurants of the East Village and Gaslamp neighborhoods. *Info*: 675 L St. Tel 619/231-6664. www.omnihotels.com.

Porto Vista Hotel $$

This hotel in vibrant Little Italy has 190 mid-century style rooms and five suites. There's valet parking, a restaurant, and a great rooftop deck with wonderful views. *Info*: 1835 Columbia St. Tel. 619/544-0164. www.portovistasd.com.

Mudville Flats $$

San Diego is known for its Craftsman homes. This boutique hotel in East Village was built in 1905, and you can rent one of the apartments here and be surrounded by Craftsman touches like lovely wood details and clawfoot tubs. California King size beds, large televisions, and WiFi add to the experience. You'll also have your own fully equipped kitchen, which makes longer stays more comfortable. A unique experience. *Info*: 747 10th Ave. Tel. 619/232-4045. www.mudvilleflats.com.

Gaslamp Plaza $$

This 1913 building was the city's first high-rise with 11 floors. Rooms, named after famous authors, are standard, but the common areas feature lots of marble and brass elevator doors. Nice rooftop deck. There are 64 rooms (some of which are timeshares). Good location near many restaurants, nightlife venues, and the Convention Center. *Info*: 520 E. Gaslamp. Tel. 619/232-9500. www.gaslampplaza.com.

Hotel Indigo $$

Going to see the Padres play baseball at Petco Park? This is your choice as the hotel overlooks the stadium. Many rooms have views of the field. Good location in the East Village/Gaslamp section of Downtown. It's pet friendly and environmentally friendly. You can drink and dine next to a firepit at Level 9 Rooftop Bar. *Info*: 509 9th Ave. Tel. 619/727-4000. www.hotelinsd.com.

La Pensione $$

You'll be within walking distance of restaurants, boutiques, bars, and cafes in the fun Little Italy neighborhood. You can choose a room with a queen bed or the larger double queen rooms. There are two onsite restaurants: Caffe Italian and Napizza Pizzeria. If you have a car, there is limited underground parking. *Info*: 606 W. Date St. Tel. 619/236-8000. www.lapensionehotel.com.

HI Hostel San Diego Downtown $

Hostelling International San Diego Downtown is located in the Gaslamp Quarter. Casual eateries and nightlife are conveniently located within walking distance. The hostel offers dorm and private rooms. There's free WiFi, coffee and tea, and breakfast. The hostel organizes tours, happy hours, pub-crawls, and occasional live music events. The budget choice Downtown. *Info*: 521 Market St. Tel. 619/525-1531. www.hihostels.com.

Coronado
Hotel del Coronado $$$
Get out your wallet for one of San Diego's best-known and most expensive destination hotels. The Victorian structure dates back to the 19th century and has an incredible beachfront location. The complex is spread over 28 acres and also includes the following options:
* Beach Village: Oceanfront enclave offering luxurious cottages and villas.
* Cabanas: Large contemporary oceanview rooms.

The complex has several restaurants, spas, boutiques, and beach rental shops. *Info*: 1500 Orange Ave. Tel. 619/435-6611. www.hoteldel.com.

Villa Capri by the Sea $-$$
Definitely *not* the Hotel del Coronado, but not everyone wants to spend the money necessary to stay at "The Del." You can't miss the large neon sign for this funky hotel. Great location, plenty of parking, and a fun vibe make this a good choice while staying in Coronado. *Info*: 1417 Orange Ave. Tel. 619/435-4137. www.villacapribythesea.com.

Old Town
Cosmopolitan Hotel $$
For a true Old Town experience, check into this 10-room historic hotel in the heart of the Old Town State Historic Park. The 19th-century hotel has modern amenities, but does have period touches such as clawfoot tubs and antique furniture. Unique! *Info*: 2660 Calhoun St. Tel. 619/297-1874. www.oldtowncosmopolitan.com

Inland Neighborhoods
Lafayette Hotel $$-$$$
There aren't a lot of hotels in the inland neighborhoods. Many who visit tend to stay at short-term rentals. This North Park hotel and swim club opened in the 1940s and was quite the destination for Hollywood celebrities. Updated, it's popular for its lively Olympic-size pool and renovated guestrooms, suites, and private bungalows. *Info*: 2223 El Cajon Blvd. Tel. 619/296-2101. www.lafayettehotelsd.com.

Ocean Beach/Point Loma
The Inn at Sunset Cliffs $$$
Get your chill on at this incredible mid-century hotel on a cliff overlooking the ocean. The view from the pool here is worth the price. The 24 rooms were built in the 1950s and updated in 2018. The large deck makes it the perfect place to watch the sunset over the Pacific Ocean. *Info*: 1370 Sunset Cliffs Blvd. Tel. 619/222-7901. www.innatsunsetcliffs.com.

Humphreys Half Moon Inn $$$
This inn features waterfront and marina views on Shelter Island. An added bonus is that all rooms have microwaves and refrigerators. This is a great place to enjoy the sunset at the hotel restaurant. The big attraction is Humphreys Concerts by the Bay at the outdoor stage on the water. Packages allow you to stay at the hotel and have VIP seating for concerts featuring some of the best-known entertainers. *Info*: 2303 Shelter Island. Tel. 619/224-3411. www.halfmooninn.com.

Ocean Beach Hostel (Samesun) $
Ocean Beach is known for its laid-back style and diverse visitors. This hostel, with its iconic rooftop peace sign, feels a bit counterculture, but is comfortable for all who want to experience the Southern California beach life. You'll find Californian surfers here, but also plenty of international visitors looking for that quintessential SoCal experience. *Info*: 4961 Newport Ave. (Ocean Beach). Tel. 619/376-6477. www.samesun.com.

The Pearl $$
Lots of repeat visitors at this Mid-Century Modern hotel with modern amenities in the center of Point Loma. The 23 rooms are arranged around the oyster-shaped pool. Dine at the restaurant (they play classic movies on the wall overlooking the pool and restaurant) or sip a cocktail at the poolside bar. Although not on the water it's within walking distance to the beach. *Info*: 1410 Rosecrans St. (Point Loma). Tel. 619/226-6100. www.thepearlsd.com.

Beach Communities
ITH Beach Bungalow Surf Hostel $
This hostel is located on the Pacific Beach Boardwalk overlooking the ocean. There are several room options including coed dorm, female-only, and private rooms (with private bathrooms). There are daily social events on the large outdoor deck where guests can socialize, check out the waves, and soak up the sunshine. Surfboard, wetsuit, and bike rentals are available. *Info*: 707 Reed Ave. (Pacific Beach). Tel. 858/412-5878. www.ithhostels.com.

Pacific Terrace $$$
Perched on a bluff overlooking the ocean on the northern end of Pacific Beach, this 73-room hotel has a great location with many restaurants within easy walking distance. Head to the beach or chill out at the pool. *Info*: 610 Diamond St. (Pacific Beach). Tel. 858/581-3500. www.pacificterrace.com.

Paradise Point $$$

Right on Mission Bay, this hotel and spa is spread out over 44 acres and features several pools, waterfalls, and ponds. Good for families as there are water sports rentals, miniature golf, Ping-Pong, and tennis courts. The complex is just a 10-minute drive from the San Diego Airport. *Info*: 1404 Vacation Rd. (Mission Bay). Tel. 877/422-9436. www.paradisepoint.com.

Tower23 $$$

Named after the lifeguard tower 23 outside the hotel on Pacific Beach, this boutique hotel offers luxury on the beach with modern design and high-end amenities. Most rooms have a view of the ocean. You can head to the rooftop deck and take in the sunset. Excellent on-site restaurant. *Info*: 723 Felspar St. (Pacific Beach). Tel. 858/270-2323. www.t23hotel.com.

Bahia Resort $$

Tucked away on 14 acres in Mission Bay, the Bahia is just a short distance from the lively Belmont Park amusement park. The lush property is family friendly and reasonably priced. California cuisine and craft cocktails are served at the restaurant and poolside bar. *Info*: 998 W. Mission Bay Dr. (Mission Bay). Tel. 858/488-0551. www.bahiahotel.com.

Crystal Pier $$-$$$

These cottages draw repeat visitors who enjoy the central Pacific Beach location and relaxed vibe. They all have private decks, kitchenettes, and a parking space. Nice place to check out and participate in beach life. *Info*: 4500 Ocean Blvd. (Pacific Beach). Tel. 800/748-5894. www.crystalpier.com.

La Jolla
The Lodge at Torrey Pines $$$

This Arts and Crafts hotel is located on cliffs overlooking the Pacific Ocean. Amenities include the Torrey Pines Golf Course, a spa, and access to hiking trails in the State Natural Reserve. Also here is the elegant restaurant **A.R. Valentien** ($$$) with breathtaking views from its patio. *Info*: 11480 N. Torrey Pines Rd. (La Jolla). Tel. 858/453-4420. www.thelodgetorreypines.com.

Hotel La Jolla $$-$$$

Sweeping ocean views from this modern high-rise hotel that's part of the Curio Collection by Hilton. It's a 10-minute walk to the beach, but you can swim in the heated pool instead. It will take you five minutes to drive to La Jolla Village. There's also a 24-hour fitness center, restaurant, and bar. *Info*: 7955 La Jolla Shores Dr. Tel. 858/551-3600. www.hotellajolla.com.

La Jolla Riviera Inn $$
Staying in La Jolla can be quite expensive, so this hotel located in a former apartment building is a good choice if you're looking to cut costs. Perfect for families as rooms have kitchens, dining areas, and living rooms (with fold-out couches). An added bonus is the small, heated pool. *Info*: 2031 Paseo Dorado. Tel. 858/224-7600. www.lajollarivierainn.com.

HOTEL CIRCLE

Hotel Circle is a cluster of hotels located off I-8 between I-5 and California Route 163 in the Mission Valley neighborhood. All the major sights of San Diego are easily accessible from these hotels by car. If you're not looking for nightlife or to stay Downtown, this is a good choice. These hotels are especially popular with families. You can book through the Hotel Circle website www.hotelcircle.net.

Some of the hotels here include:
- Comfort Inn
- Double Tree
- Motel 6
- Extended Stay
- Kings Inn
- Ramada.

10. Shopping

Shopping in San Diego ranges from your typical malls (where you might not even feel like you left home) to interesting and funky boutiques and shops. Here are some of our favorite shopping destinations.

Downtown
Bottlecraft
San Diego is known for its craft breweries and this beer shop and tasting room in Little Italy showcases hundreds of craft beers in bottles, cans, and on tap. Knowledgable and friendly bartenders will help you find the perfect choice to drink at the bar or to take home. There's also a selection of wine, cider, and kombucha (fermented, lightly effervescent tea) available. *Info*: 2252 India St. (between Ivy and Juniper). Tel. 619/487-9493. Open daily noon-8pm. There are other locations in North Park at 3007 University Ave. Tel. 619/501-1177 and in the Liberty Public Market at 2820 Historic Decatur Rd. (Liberty Station). Tel 619/269-5945. www.bottlecraftbeer.com.

Atomic Bazaar
You'll need to call ahead to make an appointment to visit this warehouse in Little Italy. It's stocked with a unique selection of high-end Mid-Century Modern vintage furniture and accessories. *Info*: 2400 Kettner Blvd. Tel 619/534-8397. www.theatomicbazaar.com.

Little Italy Design District
You'll find galleries, boutiques, furniture shops, and shops selling vintage stuff in this design district located on Kettner Blvd. and India St. between Hawthorn St. and Laurel St.

LITTLE ITALY MERCADO

Come to Little Italy (W. Date St. from Kettner Blvd. to Union St.) every Saturday from 8am-2pm to walk around the Farmer's Market. You'll find fresh seafood, produce, art, crafts, and lots of food. Grab a cup of coffee and since you're in Little Italy, try a panini from Seb's or pesto from American Basil. You'll be walking in the sunshine, so buy some all-natural sunscreen from Yeabah. Plenty of vegetarian, vegan, and gluten-free choices.

Architectural Salvage

This interesting shop in Little Italy is a trip down memory lane for old homes and buildings. Gorgeous doors, door hardware, stained glass, drawer pulls, and iron gates are just some of the items for sale here. Need a clawfoot tub? You'll find one here! *Info*: 2401 Kettner Blvd. (at W. Kalmia St.). Tel. 619/696-1313. Closed Mon. www.architecturalsalvagesd.com.

Seaport Village

A bit touristy, but this collection of 50 shops and galleries on the bay Downtown has something for everyone. Home accessories, jewelry, beach wear, local art, and plenty of restaurants for all budgets. There's live music on weekends. The adjoining Headquarters entertainment complex adds to the appeal. *Info*: Downtown on West Harbor Dr. and Pacific Hwy. (adjacent to Embarcadero Park North). Open daily 11am-7pm (hours vary by shop and restaurant). www.seaportvillage.com.

Inland

Village Hat Shop

Fedoras, top hats, bowlers, berets...you name it. Great selection of hats for women, men, and for all seasons. This is the kind of specialty shop you'd expect to find in Hillcrest. *Info*: 3821 4th Ave. Tel. 619/683-5533. Open daily. They also have locations at 3443 India St., Seaport Village at 853 W. Harbor Dr. and Pacific Beach at 979 Garnet Ave. villagehatshop.com.

Verbatim Books

Some independent bookstores still thrive even in the face of online booksellers and big box stores. This small store in North Park stocks used and rare books along with hundreds by local and Southern Californian authors. *Info*: 3793 30th St. Tel. 619/501-7466. Open daily. www.verbatim-books.com.

Buffalo Exchange

Fifth Avenue in Hillcrest is known for its collection of vintage shops. This resale shop features recycled clothes and accessories. You most likely will not empty your wallet as the average cost of an item here is about $4. *Info*: 3862 5th Ave. Tel. 619/298-4411. Open daily. There's also a location in Pacific Beach at 1079 Garnet Ave. www.buffaloexchange.com.

Pigment

This fabulous North Park boutique began as a shop to support local artists. It's expanded to include jewelry, household goods, and gifts. It has a Plant Bar where you can create a terrarium with succulents and cacti. Don't forget to pick up a macramé plant hanger. *Info*: 3801 30th St. Tel. 619/501-6318. Open daily. There are also locations in Point Loma at 2885 Perry Rd. and in Del Mar at 3715 Caminito Ct. www.shoppigment.com.

Bine and Vine Bottle Shop

In the heart of Normal Heights, this shop will meet all your wine and beer needs. Local and international craft beer, wine, cider, sake, gourmet soda, and artisan chocolate are all in stock. Knowledgeable and helpful staff. *Info*: 3334 Adams Ave. Tel. 619/795-2463. Open daily. bineandvine.com.

Sea Junk

You'll find this fascinating shop where Mission Hills meets Old Town. For more than 30 years, the Maidhof Brothers have sold nautical antiques like lamps, lanterns, instruments, furniture, portholes, and blueprints. This store reminds you that you're never too far from the water in San Diego. *Info*: 1891 San Diego Ave. Tel. 800/732-5865. Closed Sun. www.seajunk.com.

Bazaar del Mundo

This complex of shops is located on a street just outside the Old Town State Historic Park. You'll find colorful pottery, textiles, clothing, and jewelry all celebrating Mexican culture. *Info*: 4133 Taylor St. (near Sunset St.) Tel. 619/296-3161. Open daily. www.bazaardelmundo.com.

Ocean Beach, Point Loma and the Beach Communities

Vignettes

Antique, vintage, repurposed, and reclaimed furniture, jewelry, art, and more at this shop in Ocean Beach. If you can't find what you want here, there are several antique and vintage shops along Newport Avenue. *Info*: 4828 Newport Ave. (Ocean Beach). Tel. 619/223-6170. Open daily. www.vignettesdecor.com.

The Black

Peace, man! This store is the essence of Ocean Beach. A little bit hippie, a little bit counterculture, and a lot eclectic. Breathe in the incense while you shop for caps, T-shirts, gifts, jewelry, smoking pipes, and (of course) candles and incense. *Info*: 5017 Newport Ave. (Ocean Beach). Tel. 619/222-5498. Closed Sun. www.theblackoceanbeach.com.

Sun Diego Boardshop
Come here for all your surfer needs. Fullsuits, longboards, clothing (especially hoodies), and even accessories for snowboarding. *Info*: 3126 Mission Blvd. (Mission Beach). Tel. 858/866-0108. Open daily. www.sundiego.com.

Mission Surf
San Diego's first surf shop has been near the pier in Pacific Beach for over 50 years. Rent a surfboard, boogie board, wetsuit, skateboard, and more. If you want to immerse yourself in surf culture, you can rent one of their vacation rental apartments located above the surf shop. *Info*: 4320 Mission Blvd. (Pacific Beach). Tel. 858/483-8837. Open daily. www.missionsurf.com.

Pennywise Books
We love these small, independently owned bookstores. You're going to be spending some time in the sand while in the beach communities, so why not pop into this store in Pacific Beach and select a used paperback to read while relaxing in the sun? *Info*: 1331 Garnet Ave. (Pacific Beach). Tel. 858/270-1640. Closed Sun and Mon. www.pennywisebooks.info.

La Jolla
This coastal community is a shopper's paradise.

For fashion, head to **Girard Avenue**, where you'll find chain retail stores along with high-end local boutiques. You can also explore shops selling books (**D.G. Wills** at 7461), jewelry (**Bowers** at 7860), home goods (**Design Studio West** at 7422), furniture (**Nativa Interiors** at 7770), and antiques (**Girard Ave Marketplace** at 7505).

On **Prospect Street**, there are many specialty shops along with quite a few galleries showcasing art, sculpture, photography, and crafts. Don't miss the **National Geographic Fine Art Gallery** at 1205 Prospect St. with a wonderful collection of nature photography. Tel. 619/568-6790. Open daily. www.natgeofineart.com.

Bring your credit cards as these are mostly expensive stores.

11. Planning Your Trip/ Practical Matters

Arriving

San Diego International Airport (SAN) is three miles northwest of Downtown San Diego. Its location makes it convenient for travelers to get to where they are staying. A taxi ride from the airport to Downtown hotels is between $15 and $20. www.san.org.

Some travelers fly into the following airports:
Tijuana, Mexico (TIJ): 23 miles/37 kilometers
Santa Ana (SNA): 87 miles/140 kilometers
Ontario, CA (ONT): 115 miles/185 kilometers
Los Angeles (LAX): 125 miles/201 kilometers
Palm Springs (PSP): 146 miles/235 kilometers

The **Greyhound Bus Station** is located Downtown in East Village at 1313 National Ave. between 13th St. and 14th St.

Car Rental

All major car-rental companies operate at SAN. All pick-ups and drop-offs occur at the Consolidated Rental Car Center at 3355 Admiral Boland Way. Free shuttle busses run between the airport terminals and the Rental Car Center.

Taxis/Rideshare

If you want to take a taxi from the airport, follow the signs leading to the Transportation Plaza across from Terminals 1 and 2. For rideshare and shuttle services, also follow the signs to the Transportation Plaza.

Practical Matters

Banking & Money

Call your credit-card company or bank before you leave to tell them you'll be using your ATM or credit card outside your usual area. Many have automatic controls that can "freeze" your account if the computer program determines that there are charges outside your normal range.

ATMs (with fees, of course) are the easiest way to change money if you are visiting from outside the United States. You'll find them everywhere, including the airport.

Climate & Weather

The fabulous weather in San Diego is one of the major draws for visitors. The area enjoys 280 sunny and partly sunny days a year. Rainfall is low, averaging about 10 inches (254 mm) per year.

August is the hottest month in San Diego with an average temperature of 73°F (23°C), and the coldest is January at 57°F (14°C). July is the sunniest month with 10 daily sunshine hours. The wettest month is January with an average of 2.28 inches (58mm) of rain. The best month to swim in the ocean is August, when the average sea temperature is 68°F (20°C).

In late May and June, the marine layer rolls in and you'll likely experience what San Diegans call "May Gray" and "June Gloom." There's often a 10-15°F difference from the cooler coast to inland areas.

Average high temperature/low temperature °F and °C and days of rain:

High °F	Low °F		High °C	Low °C	Rainfall (inches)
67	51	January	20	10	2.28
67	52	February	19	11	2.04
68	55	March	20	13	2.26
70	58	April	21	14	0.75
69	60	May	21	16	0.20
71	63	June	22	17	0.09
75	66	July	24	19	0.03
77	68	August	25	20	0.09
78	67	September	26	19	0.21
76	63	October	25	17	0.44
72	56	November	22	13	1.07
67	51	December	19	10	1.31

You should check www.weather.com before you leave.

DINING PRICES

Prices for a main course:
- $$$$ Very Expensive: over $30
- $$$ Expensive: $21-$30
- $$ Moderate: $10-$20
- $ Inexpensive: under $10

Events and Festivals

January

San Diego Restaurant Week

San Diego's restaurants celebrate the local dining scene with prix-fixe menus. www.sandiegorestaurantweek.com

Farmers Insurance Open

The PGA Tour men's golf tournament at the Torrey Pines Golf Course in La Jolla. www.farmersinsuranceopen.com.

February

Museum Month

Local museums offer discounts and special events. www.sandiegomuseumcouncil.org.

Mardi Gras in the Gaslamp Quarter

Fat Tuesday celebration with parades, music, and beads in the historic Gaslamp Quarter. gaslampmardigras.com.

March

Flower Fields

Fifty acres come into bloom at the Flower Fields at Carlsbad Ranch from March to May. www.theflowerfields.com.

April

San Diego Crew Classic

Regatta event brings rowers from across the country to Crown Point Shores on Mission Bay. crewclassic.org.

Padres Baseball

Major League Baseball at Petco Park from April to October. www.mlb.com/padres.

May

Old Town Fiesta Cinco de Mayo

Celebrate Mexican culture with music and food in Old Town, the birthplace of San Diego. www.oldtownsandiegoguide.com.

June

Rock 'n' Roll Marathon

Bands, costumes, parties, and, of course, running. www.runrocknroll.com.

San Diego County Fair

San Diego's county fair features food, livestock, garden shows, carnival rides, and concerts at the Del Mar Fairgrounds. www.sdfair.com.

Shakespeare Festival

Shakespeare productions performed at The Old Globe Theatre in Balboa Park from June to September. www.theoldglobe.org.

July
Pride
A celebration of San Diego's LGBTQ community with a parade and festival. www.sdpride.org.
Del Mar Racing
Thoroughbred racing at the Del Mar Thoroughbred Club from July to September. www.dmtc.com.
Comic-Con
The largest comics and pop culture event in the United States attracts celebrities and fans of comic books, movie memorabilia, and pop culture. www.comic-con.org.
September
World Body Surfing Championships
Surfers from around the world compete at the Oceanside Pier and Beach. visitoceanside.org.
MCAS Miramar Air Show
Air show featuring the best military and civilian pilots in the world at the Marine Corps Air Station in Miramar. www.miramarairshow.com.
October
Kids Free
Kids eat, stay, visit, and play for free at over 100 museums, attractions, tours, hotels, and restaurants. www.sandiego.org.
November
San Diego Beer Week
This 10-day festival highlights San Diego's award-winning craft beer, breweries, and pubs. www.sdbw.org
Wine & Food Festival
A five-day wine and culinary extravaganza, held throughout Downtown. www.sandiegowineclassic.com.
December
Parade of Lights
Festively decorated boats are featured in this holiday parade on the waterfront. www.sdparadeoflights.org.

Internet Access/WiFi
WiFi is available at most hotels, bars, cafes, and restaurants.

Packing/Dress
Never pack prescription drugs, eyeglasses, or valuables in your checked suitcase. Carry them on. Don't ruin your trip by having to lug around bulky suitcases. San Diego is quite casual. It's okay to dress casually for dinner, except in more expensive restaurants.

Postal Services

The main post office is located downtown at 815 E St. It's open Mon-Fri 9am-5pm. If you need a stamp, many souvenir shops sell them with postcards.

Public Transportation

Metropolitan Transit System (MTS) is the city's public transportation network. Extensive bus and trolley lines serve the entire county. The trolley has three color-coded lines (Blue, Green, and Orange), all of which serve the central city. The Blue line extends all the way south to the Mexican border. The bus line can be confusing, but you can plan your route at www.sdmts.com. A single route on a bus line or trolley costs $2.50 ($1.25 for seniors and disabled). A one-day pass is $8 if you do not have a Compass Card (which most visitors do not).

Restrooms

There aren't a lot of public restrooms (toilets). If you need to go, your best bet is to head (no pun intended) to the nearest bar or café. It's considered good manners to purchase something if you use the restroom.

Smoking

Smoking is prohibited in hotels, restaurants, bars, clubs, museums, and on public transportation. Smoking outdoors is also restricted in certain areas.

Tipping

San Diego is a tourist destination, and many workers rely on tips to make a living. Most people tip 20% at restaurants. If you are visiting from outside the United States, know that it is extremely rare for the tip to be included in your bill.

Tourist Information

Tourism Information Centers are located at:
San Diego: 996 N. Harbor Dr. (at the Embarcadero). Tel. 619/236-1242. Open daily 9am-4pm. www.sandiegovisit.org.
Coronado: 1100 Orange Ave. Tel. 619/437-8788. Open daily 10am-5pm. www.coranadovisitorcenter.com.

Websites

- Europe Made Easy Travel Guides: www.eatndrink.com
- City of San Diego: www.sandiegovisit.org.
- California: www.visitcalifornia.com

12. Index

Palm Springs Made Easy

Your Guide to the Coachella Valley, Joshua Tree, Hi-Desert, Salton Sea, Idyllwild, and more!

Palm Springs has something for everyone. If you love nature, there are spectacular hiking trails to explore, and the breathtaking Aerial Tramway. If art is your passion, take in the Palm Springs Art Museum, or the Uptown District's galleries.

How about architecture? After all, you'll be in the heart of Mid-Century Modern and Spanish Revival! And when you need to refuel, take your pick from the many friendly (and festive!) restaurants and bars all over downtown, and throughout the Coachella Valley.

From the stark beauty of Joshua Tree National Park to exciting gay nightlife and resorts—including insider tips on cafes, restaurants, and shops—this concise little pocket guide will help you plan your trip with confidence. However short your stay, it's all you'll need to make your visit enjoyable, memorable—and easy!

For a list of all Europe Made Easy travel guides, and to purchase our books, visit www.eatndrink.com